HOW DO YOU MEASURE UP?

MELANIE D. WEST

FOREWORD BY DR. ALTHERIA W. JONES

LOVE CHECK
Copyright © 2020 by Melanie D. West. All Rights Reserved.

No part of this publication may be reproduced, stored, or transmitted in any form or by any means – except brief quotations in printed reviews, without the prior written permission of the copyright owner.

Cover Design: Melanie D. West (KingdomKreatives.com)
Editing: Melanie D. West & Dr. Michael Jones
Foreword: Dr. Altheria W. Jones

ISBN: 978-0-578-80691-4 (paperback)

All scripture quotations, unless indicated, are taken from the English Standard Version (ESV) of the Holy Bible. Copyright © 2001 by Crossway, a publishing ministry of Good News Publishers. Used by permission. All rights reserved.

Verses marked NIV are from the New International Version of the Bible, Copyright © 1973, 1978, 1984, 2011 by Biblica, Inc®. Used by permission of Zondervan. All rights reserved.

Verses marked ERV are from the Easy-to-Read Version of the Bible. Copyright © 2006 by Bible League International®. Used by permission. All rights reserved.

Verses marked MSG are from THE MESSAGE, Copyright © 1993, 2002, 2018 by Eugene H. Peterson. Used by permission of NavPress. All rights reserved. Represented by Tyndale House Publishers, Inc.

This publication is designed to provide information about the subject matter covered. It is sold with the understanding that the author and contributors are not rendering any professional services. If you require expert advice, you should seek a professional.

Printed in the United States of America

DEDICATION

This book is dedicated to my mother, Pearl (who truly is a jewel), and all the other beautiful souls out there with a heart of gold – those who have consistently loved when loving was difficult, when love was necessary, when love was unpopular – some of which I've had the pleasure of meeting or are still part of my life today. You are truly the hands and heart of God in the earth. Love uplifts, strengthens, transforms and heals – and you are, no doubt, a healer. This book is also dedicated to all those who have ever felt unloved, undervalued, unseen or unheard. Those who have experienced trials that made them question their relationships, friendships or faith. Life has a way of rocking us to our core at times, but we are never beyond the love and saving grace of God. You are loved – unconditionally, relentlessly, forever!

ACKNOWLEDGMENTS
Thank You...

To God, the Creator and Originator of Love. It's an honor to know You, learn from You and share You with the world.

To my family, some of my biggest cheerleaders and supporters, I couldn't do this without you. Special thanks to my mom, for her wisdom, prayers and best wishes in all my endeavors; my sister, Keri, for her invaluable hands-on support, encouragement and push to finish this book; and my niece Shanaye for her behind-the-scenes work to help me gather info to write this book.

To the Free Gospel Deliverance Temple family, the house and leadership that introduced me to Christ and helped to birth my ministry and spiritual gifts. You have loved and supported me through the years. I love you all.

To Freddie Simmons, for your constant friendship, prayers and inspiration. Ours has truly been a divine connection, and our years of ministry together have been invaluable training ground for new levels.

To Prophetess Cynthia Rawles, for encouraging me, speaking into my life and sparking my ministry endeavors.

To Drs. Michael and Altheria Jones, for their patience, time and willingness to assist me. Thanks, Dr. Mike, for your theological expertise in helping me to achieve biblical accuracy in the writing of this book. Dr. Altheria, you are a gem and I appreciate you for agreeing to write the foreword of this book.

To Pastor Marvin and 1st Lady Terry Wilson; Toyer and Tanya Blake; and Maurice and Sherita Wilson, for their time, transparency and willingness to share invaluable wisdom and a small window into their years of marriage. You all are proof that 1 Corinthians 13 love is abundant and possible, even in marriage.

To every friend and supporter, who has loved, prayed, listened, advised, assisted, inspired and poured into me or contributed in some way to the birthing of this book, you rock!

TABLE OF CONTENTS

Foreword i
Chapter 1. Intro: Got Love? 1
- The Purpose Of This Book 2

Chapter 2. What Is Love To You? 5
Chapter 3. The Love Chapter: 1 Corinthians 13 11
- What Agape Love Is Not 14
- What Agape Love Is 20
- What Agape Love Does 32
- 1 Corinthians 13 Love Test 41

Chapter 4. Jesus: The Blueprint 43
Chapter 5. Mr. & Mrs. Right? 73
- Maurice & Sherita Wilson 78
- Pastor Marvin & 1st Lady Terry Wilson 90
- Toyer & Tanya Blake 100

Chapter 6. Decisions, Decisions 125
- Part 1: What Would You Do? (Quiz) 125
- Part 2: What Would Love Do? (Assessment) ... 132

Appendix: Resources 141
- Got Christ? 141
- Saved and Seeking to Go Deeper? 144
- 13 Love Bytes: God's Love
  Revealed In Scripture 148
- 101 Ways to Love 150

FOREWORD

As an ordained Minister of the Gospel, Christian Counselor and retired public high school Media Specialist, I have had the pleasure to know the author, Melanie West, for many years. We have ministered alongside each other, sharing in love and grace both theological and philosophical ideas from a Christian perspective -- which has definitely raised the calm in her to create such a 'blessed work' on Agape Love and its application to God's people.

Written from a Christian perspective, and personal life experiences, dealing with love, pain, etc., Melanie West demonstrates the supremacy of love throughout.

Love Check is such a valuable tool that it can be used by all believers, on all levels. The reading will also encourage and touch the heart of the non-believer in hopes that they will desire to follow after God and seek His everlasting love.

Because God desires and mandates that we love every individual that we come to know, whether good, bad or indifferent, we are supposed to pour out agape love towards them, as Christ does for us. Even though at times, it's very difficult to do, because we live in a sin-cursed world, yet the author makes it so surreal in the creative writing and delivery until you don't want to put the book to rest.

Altheria Washington Jones, DMin

CHAPTER 1

GOT LOVE?

Have you ever wondered what a world without hate would look like – a world **full** of love? If we just look around us, look at the daily news, look at the wars and conflicts around the world, look at the needs of the people everywhere – the despair, the addictions, the heartaches, the crime, the injustices, the religious feuds and all that is wrong in the world… what do we really see? A truth I've discovered that is overwhelmingly evident in all peoples, in all parts of the world: People just wanna be loved. I believe that Love is the universal answer to the problem that ails us all. As cliché as it may sound, truly, what the world needs NOW is Love. There isn't a racism problem without first being a love problem. There isn't a crime problem without first being a love problem. There isn't a corruption problem without first being a love problem. Somewhere, at the root of it all, love is lacking. Love is misrepresented. Love has often been put on the shelf and some other trinket put in its place.

And though I'm sure we could each come up with our own little list of people we call "haters," and we could name at least a few people who we say don't know how to love, don't know what real love is, and who are likely contributing to this love dilemma in the world... guess what? The real truth is that it has to start with you. It has to start with me. One person at a time. One heart embracing another. One light sparking another. Just one. Be a calm presence of love. Let your heart shine like a beacon. It is surprising what a difference one light can make.

THE PURPOSE OF THIS BOOK

Much of the content of this book is written from a Christian perspective, because I am a Christian. But these principles, thoughts and actions can be applied to practically anyone, in any walk of life and in practically any religion. If you are reading this book, you are at least **trying** to see where you (or those in your life) stand when it comes to having the God-kind of love (agape), are seeking to love better or love more, and/or have a sincere desire to represent God better by exemplifying the primary fruit of His Spirit. You want to do your part to add more love to the world. So I applaud you for that and I'm sure God is pleased with you and me for trying to improve our love walk. Now, first things first: In order for this to work, we've got to take a deep and honest look at ourselves and where we are currently – the good, the bad and the ugly. We've also got to draw closer to God. He is that Constant. He is the full embodiment of Love, and if we want to fill up on love, He is our primary Source. We cannot love others without first **being** loved or being **filled** with love ourselves. We need more of His Spirit! I invite you to go on a journey with me, as we delve deeper into this wonder we call Love.

CHAPTER 2
WHAT IS LOVE TO YOU?

Pause and ask yourself that question. Think about it for just a moment before continuing...

Dictionary.com lists more than 10 definitions for love and most of them describe love as some type of **feeling**. They're all perfectly good definitions, but love is so much more. From the super-saved to the unsaved, we all have our own theories about love, largely colored by our own personal experiences or things we've witnessed and heard from others. I see love as an ocean (endless, overflowing and buoyant); as oxygen (that sustains, resuscitates, revives and serves as a lifeline); as light (warm, glowing and piercing through darkness); and as the very nature and acts of God... because it's too great a thing to be described in small terms. And love, quite literally, is big, wide, deep, powerful, and most definitely an action word. The beautiful feelings associated with love are nothing if they don't move you to act on them. Love causes you to water the object of your affection and to, yourself, become better and do better.

I have always had a pretty natural inclination to being kind, loving and forgiving. But let me be honest: What I have found now is that, that natural tendency doesn't come so easy anymore; maintaining my love walk has become more of a challenge in the last few years. It's like I have to consciously work to maintain it now. Don't get me wrong: I am still a kind, loving and forgiving person; but where it once was practically effortless, there are times and certain situations where I **really** have to work at it. I am reminded of what Paul said in Romans 7:21: "When I want to do right, evil lies close at hand."

The things you pray for often become areas of great testing. And, no doubt, praying for a heart like God's means you're going to need to be even kinder, even more loving, and even more forgiving. But that also means that in order to develop that kind of aptitude and capacity for love, you will likely experience warfare in that area and even be exposed to more difficult people and circumstances that force you to grow in that same area. The more you go through, the more you grow through. It is NOT easy, I promise you. It must be an intentional act and a commitment to the process, to do better and to be better. The reward for loving is more love, so it's worth it.

Get Uncomfortable

Our natural minds and our human nature make us want to do what's easiest, most convenient and most comfortable when it comes to love. And to be honest, this is something I've had to press through too. You see, my human nature makes me wanna clap back when someone

LOVE CHECK – What is Love to You?

says something off the wall to me. My human nature makes me wanna hold a grudge when someone hurts my feelings. My human nature makes me wanna cut people off when they continually misuse, abuse or disrespect me. My human nature makes me wanna do people exactly how they do me when they mistreat me; we even rationalize foolishly, knowing that's not what God meant by the biblical adage, "You reap what you sow." We would like to believe the golden rule says, "Do to others as they do to you" instead of what it actually says: "Do to others as you would **have** them do to you." (Luke 6:31, NIV). Huge difference.

We would like to think that there's a cap on the number of times we're supposed to forgive someone. I mean, our finite minds can't even begin to grasp the biblical idea of forgiving someone 70x7 times (490 times)! Is that even possible? How much easier is it to clap back when insulted, hold a grudge when offended, attack when teased, hate when hurt, etc? We want so badly to retaliate against those who cause us harm. It just makes logical sense.

Now, while we should assertively speak up for ourselves and defend ourselves against assault, God generally wants us to take the gentler approach to conflict – to fight evil with good, fight hate with love, and fight to attain and maintain peace by returning soft answers and peaceful responses to argumentative and belligerent people. "Blessed are the peacemakers," remember? We can't overlook the part in the Bible that says, "...Vengeance is Mine, I will repay, says the Lord" (Romans 12:19). That's His job, to repay those who do us wrong, as hard as it is not to react in kind or take matters into our own hands.

This all takes work, practice, time and a conscious and intentional effort to deal with conflict in this manner. But we must "seek peace and pursue it" (Psalm 34:14). It won't happen overnight, and the best of us still struggle from time to time with keeping our composure when facing conflict.

LOVE CHECK – What is Love to You?

We're going to have to do some "breathing exercises" if we want to create and maintain a positive space. Exhale negativity, inhale positivity, and repeat. Literally and figuratively... Just breathe, pray and do your best to maintain love and peace in your space – whatever that looks like for you.

CRITICAL THINKING EXERCISE:

Think of a recent time when you were mistreated, offended or hurt by someone. Think about how you felt. Think about how you responded. Were you able to bring about or maintain an atmosphere of peace and love? How could you have handled the situation differently?

CHAPTER 3

THE LOVE CHAPTER:
1 CORINTHIANS 13

1 Corinthians 13 is **thee** love chapter. No other chapter in all of sacred scripture spells love out that clearly. I go there periodically to see how I am measuring up to God's definition of what real love is supposed to look like, sound like, act like and be like. I encourage anyone wanting to improve their love walk to do the same. It may be even more beneficial if you have someone to serve as a sounding board – to tell you if **they** think you measure up, because relationship forces you to see yourself in new ways and from other perspectives. We may not notice our own flaws or

even our own greatness, if not observed and acknowledged by those who know us best. Armed with this knowledge, these are our marching orders: To love God supremely and to love our neighbors as ourselves. The bar is set high, but we must continually strive to meet the mark. It is no easy feat for anyone, but with God's help, we can make strides and reach new heights in love.

The love defined here is a mirror image of the agape love that Christ personifies. For the full definition, we can look closely at verses 4 thru 8 of 1 Corinthians 13. But we must explore the entire chapter to see what real love is **not**, what real love **is**, what real love **does**, and how God crowns love as supreme amidst all other spiritual gifts, fruits and qualities we may have or epitomize as believers.

The Bible says in John 13:35 that people will know we are Christ's disciples, or Christians, by our love. It's the distinct and distinguishing signpost to the world that we know God, and that He lives within us, when we can truly love others. Loving God comes easier, because He's got a proven track record of being consistently faithful, present, caring, dependable, loving, merciful and just, etc. I've met some great people, and there are many great people in the world. However, people can be quite challenging at times; people can be fickle, moody, unreliable, unkind, rude, indifferent, etc., and everyone has their own unique personality. So daily, here we are trying to wade through all these different personalities in all these different bodies, yet we still have to find a way to love them like God loves us? One can get tired just thinking about that! Understand that we cannot do this on our own strength. It requires a power greater than our own; it takes God. The closer we are to God, the more of His love nature will be displayed in us.

Once you have gotten in the habit of having regular communion with God, and/or regular communion with the people in your life who also possess and operate in that God-kind of love, your love meter will reach full capacity. You can now pour His agape love out onto others, and back onto God Himself. God makes it pretty clear how to love Him in return. He simply wants us to acknowledge Him and make Him priority #1 in our lives, love Him above all else, and love others as ourselves. Loving others as ourselves is where it can get a little tricky, but here's where 1 Corinthians 13 comes into play. I like to think of this as God's Metric System. This is our outline and gauge to determine if we are really loving people the correct way, and if people are really loving us correctly.

People use that term so loosely nowadays. Everyone is quick to say, "I love you." But here's how to know if it's just lip service or the real deal. Let's explore all 13 verses of 1 Corinthians, chapter 13, in more depth.

WHAT AGAPE LOVE IS NOT

The first three verses let us know, matter-of-factly, how to spot a counterfeit or at least to know where God truly places value in service to Him. Out of all the acts we can do for God, love is supreme.

The Supremacy of Love

Verse 1:
"If I speak in the tongues of men and of angels, but have not love, I am a noisy gong or a clanging cymbal."

Eloquent speech (natural) and speaking in tongues, or your heavenly language (spiritual), may be gifts that cause us to appear deep and/or educated; people may ooh and ahh when they see us doing either of the two. That's not to say that these aren't gifts to desire, use or admire. The point here is that if love is not evident, and we're not clearly operating in love, any words (natural or spiritual) that leave our mouths are literally just a bunch of empty noise –

equivalent to the loud, crashing sound of a cymbal being struck!

Imagine for a moment an abusive husband who beats his wife on a regular basis, but then comes back to her day after day saying he's sorry. The sound of his voice and the words that he speaks to her, no matter how sincere or not, will likely come off to her like the screeching sound of someone scratching a chalkboard – annoying and undesired – and eventually she just won't believe him. Another point to drive home here is that actions speak louder than words. Love is definitely an action word. If you are **saying** you love somebody and your actions are saying something different, that's not love, my friend. No matter how well, loud or long you say it.

Verse 2:

"And if I have prophetic powers, and understand all mysteries and all knowledge, and if I have all faith, so as to remove mountains, but have not love, I am nothing."

This verse is highlighting more spiritual gifts – the gift of prophecy and the gift of faith. The Bible says that we can and should aspire to have spiritual gifts. It even says that prophecy is the gift we should most covet. The prophetic is such a highly esteemed spiritual gift. Prophetic people are often either greatly admired or envied, because they essentially have a unique and direct pipeline to God, keen sensitivity to the Spirit and voice of God, and speak on His behalf. They hear the voice of the Lord, see divine visions and dreams clearer than most and are able to understand and/or interpret what God is saying or showing. All spiritual gifts serve a great Kingdom purpose, but these gifts operate best when love is present. This verse is very blunt in saying that no matter how esteemed or affluent you are with your spiritual gifts and what great feats and exploits you may do as a result of those gifts, <u>without love</u> you are **nothing**. Ouch! Remember, God is Love. Literally, <u>without God</u>, we are nothing! John 15:5 reinforces that truth: "…Apart from Me, you can **do** nothing."

Verse 3:

"If I give away all I have, and if I deliver up my body to be burned, but have not love, I gain nothing."

Self-sacrificing deeds like being extremely and exhaustively generous and risking or giving one's life for a cause sound like very brave, heroic and praiseworthy acts of love, don't they? That's probably the automatic perception most people would have of someone doing such things. Surely they'd get major brownie points, admiration and prestige for being so giving! Why, then, would God imply here that you can do these things and not have love? Hmmm… Could it be that God looks at the heart or the motives behind such acts? Think about this for a moment: What else could make someone give away all they have, say, to charities or to the poor except it be done in the spirit of love? Could they be looking for acceptance, approval, fame or the **appearance** of love? Could it be for something as superficial as the hopes of getting a big tax write-off and subsequent return later? Why else would someone give their very life other than for the cause of love? Could they be playing the martyr and desire to be remembered as one who "loved" others enough to die for them? Could their intent have been like that of suicide bombers, who sacrifice their very lives to kill their enemies and those they hate, to initiate wars or perhaps to gain an esteemed position in the afterlife, as is their religious belief?

Now, these are merely examples and hypothetical possibilities, but God is saying in this verse that doing any types of self-sacrificing acts, no matter how great, are of no real profit to you if love is not the reason. You're essentially just going through the motions. Our works will be tested by fire, and only that done in love and for God will remain. The Bible says in 2 Corinthians 9:7 that God loves "a cheerful giver" – one who finds joy in giving and doesn't mind giving, but gives willingly from a place of love. Love gives, and not necessarily expecting anything in return. We should give in love or not at all.

WHAT AGAPE LOVE IS

Now that we have discovered what agape love is **not** from the 1st three verses of 1 Corinthians 13 (and as we'll discover further in a few more verses of this chapter), we can now explore what agape love **is**, by taking a more in-depth look at verses 4, 7 and 8. What exactly does real love look like, according to sacred scripture?

LOVE CHECK – The Love Chapter: 1 Corinthians 13

Verse 4:

"Love is patient and kind ..."

Patience truly is a virtue. Love causes you to be patient with those you love. You are able to suffer long and endure difficult moments and hard times with the ones you love, because love gives you a grace to handle it and them. Kindness in love goes without saying. Someone you love is seen as precious in your sight, and we naturally care for things and people we value, right? Even in momentary moments of anger, real love always softens and returns to kindness and tenderness towards the objects of our affection.

WHAT AGAPE LOVE IS NOT

Verse 4 (continued):

"...love does not envy or boast; it is not arrogant..."

Point number three from verse 4 begins a few more examples of what love is **not**: Love doesn't envy. There would be no need to envy someone if you truly love them. Envy is essentially coveting or desiring what someone else has. According to dictionary.com, "to envy is to feel resentful and unhappy because someone else possesses, or has achieved, what one wishes oneself to possess, or to have achieved" (Envy, n.d.). Some things we ask for and don't receive because our motives are wrong, and sometimes God **knows** better or **has** better for us. Seeing someone you love happy and blessed **should** make you happy, not envious. So check that emotion at the door, should you find yourself feeling envious.

Boasting is an action usually accompanied by pride and self-indulgence, where one speaks in an exaggerated and arrogant manner, usually about oneself. The Bible states in 1 Corinthians 1:31 that if you're gonna boast, "boast in the Lord." When we realize and acknowledge where all our blessings, skills and talents – all things good

LOVE CHECK – The Love Chapter: 1 Corinthians 13

about us and others – come from, we can humbly give God all the glory and boast in Him instead. Giving compliments is fine. Giving thanks and appreciation to God for all the good things in our lives is great. Flattery, self-aggrandizement, vanity and pride are not.

<u>Arrogance</u> tends to walk hand in hand with boasting, though it is **entirely** self-focused. Love is not arrogant. Now, let's not confuse arrogance with confidence. Confidence is a firm trust, belief and assurance; it can be quiet yet powerful, assertive yet nonabrasive, calm yet bold, strong yet humble. Confidence is more so an awareness of who you are or Whose you are and not allowing your God-given identity to be diminished or rattled by anyone or anything. Arrogance is thinking or speaking too highly of oneself, one's possessions or accomplishments in a manner that touts you as superior to others and them as inferior. We all know or have encountered that person who never ceases to pat themselves on the back, vie for a moment in the spotlight or talk about themselves

every chance they get. The Bible says in Proverbs 27:2 that you should "let another praise you, and not your own mouth; a stranger, and not your own lips." How, then, can you be expressing love, which is generally outwardly focused and selfless, if your attention and conversation is mostly on yourself? People who think too highly of themselves have a hard time submitting to or serving others. Love, on the other hand, gladly yields and freely gives.

Verse 5:

"...or rude. It does not insist on its own way; it is not irritable or resentful..."

Love is <u>not rude</u>. When you love someone, you are ruled by compassion. You're not so quick to act or react in a rude manner or speak coarse words to those you love. Even in the instance when, let's say, a loving mother inadvertently snaps at her child during a tense moment, she will always soften and welcome that child back

LOVE CHECK – The Love Chapter: 1 Corinthians 13

into her arms, because the love she has for her child doesn't want to see them hurt or upset.

By default, love causes one to be selfless, <u>not selfish</u>. Rather than a "me, me, me" mentality, you'll be more interested in making your loved ones happy and satisfied.

Love is <u>not irritable</u>. Love makes a conscious decision to be kind, gentle and patient with others in word and deed. So while the occasional mood or feelings associated with frustration may crop up from time to time, they should never trump love in action.

"By default, love causes one to be selfless, not selfish… you'll be more interested in making your loved ones happy."

Love is <u>not resentful</u>. The Oxford Dictionary Online defines "resentful" as "having or expressing bitterness or indignation at having been treated unfairly" (Resentful, n.d.). So while irritation deals with emotion more on the surface level, resentment is a deep-seated emotion that has taken root below the surface, usually over the course of time. I don't know about you, but I'm not one to be angry or hold grudges for long, especially toward those I love. It's just my divine makeup, but I know everyone is not wired that way. Wounds from those we love are the most painful and hardest to comprehend, so that's not to say that initial feelings of anger, frustration or disappointment aren't warranted. However, bitterness is a lingering poison, one that we've allowed to fester and grow.

The Bible teaches that we should be slow to anger, but quick to repent and forgive. If we strive to exhibit this type of behavior instead of popping off and/or holding onto every little thing that offends, hurts or irritates, we don't give bitterness the chance to set in. And though it's often difficult to simply forgive and forget, depending on the circumstances, it *is* possible when we intentionally pause to calm ourselves (perhaps pray too), allow the initial emotions to pass, think things through, and then respond (not react) with love. Now, some things are just gonna take time. Some offenses and infractions against us scar us in such a way that only time, prayer, the Spirit of God and our absolute willingness and commitment to forgive will allow healing and recovery.

Transparent Moment: I was once confronted with a betrayal that was so painful, the only way I could cope was to bury it. The person admitted the betrayal, so that counted for something. Though my emotions internally were raging all over the place, I listened and then excused myself so I could try to grasp what I was told and get my feelings under control because I could feel them reaching a boiling point. After a few hours in solitude, trying to make sense of it all though I couldn't, I let my emotions run wild because I promise you I needed that release. So there I was battling from one extreme to another of screaming to crying to silence to praying to cursing (keeping it real) – and still there were no answers. How was I gonna get through **this**? When I tell you I was on an emotional rollercoaster, that is an understatement. In spite of all of this, there was this overwhelming press in my spirit (obviously from God) for me to be obedient to the very thing I've been trying to live by all this time – agape love, which commands us to love at all times and forgive in every situation. So my flesh was at war with the Spirit of God on the inside of me for sure.

Eventually, but without much delay, I made my way back to the one who had betrayed me and literally forced myself to say those words, "I forgive you." I couldn't even believe what I heard myself say. But I knew that I had to do it, because God was nudging me to and I strive to obey Him to the best of my ability. I didn't linger and I didn't really say much more beyond that, and then I left their presence. I didn't allow any additional dialogue, though they apologized again, because I wasn't sure I could handle it at that moment. All I knew was that I had to be obedient. I was enraged but the love I felt was still there. I'm talking about real, agape love. It's stronger than betrayal, hate, death... and even though I felt like part of me died that day, I understood how real love was and is.

I said all that to say this: Forgiveness isn't always easy; it's even harder when the perpetrators don't apologize or correct their behavior. Though I had spoken those words out of my mouth, I continually prayed to God, cried and struggled many days and nights thereafter for my spirit, body and mind to line up with the words I had spoken. It didn't come easy, and it was a fight every day, but I was determined not to allow myself to become bitter. I didn't want to become the mean-spirited, hateful, vengeful person I had seen others become. Unforgiveness is a beast and bitterness is a poison; both are toxic. If unchecked, they will constantly be at war with love, at war with you and could negatively affect your relationships, your prayers, your life and even your health.

I buried the pain of betrayal initially because I don't think I could've functioned too well otherwise, to keep it at the surface or wear it on my sleeve, so to speak. I talked and cried and prayed my way through. I worked and sang and read my way through. I laughed and journaled and ate my way through. I kept busy with things and people I loved, and my relationship with God became stronger.

We all have ways to self-medicate through pain. I'm just grateful that God has been my strongest medicine – and eventually my Healer. It was during painful moments like these that God downloaded His love to me the most, in many different ways. By Him filling me up with His love, I have learned to love Him, others and myself more. So I encourage you, if you are "going through" something like this, where you feel like forgiveness is difficult or seemingly impossible, "keep going." You can make it.

Verse 6:
"...it does not rejoice at wrongdoing..."

While love is patient, kind, forgiving and all those beautiful things we've already mentioned, it is not a pass to do wrong to others because we know they will love and forgive us; neither is it a pass to accept or allow mistreatment from others just because we love them and must forgive them as God commands. While love doesn't condemn and beat someone over the head for doing something wrong, there's nothing wrong with at least addressing the behavior, being assertive and/or trying to take corrective actions. Love <u>doesn't glorify wrongdoing</u>, because anything we praise will be magnified, intensified and strengthened. The Bible says that God is love, God is just, God is merciful, etc., but the Bible also teaches that God hates sin – even though He loves the sinner. Because God will forgive us of our sins, are we therefore free to sin without consequence? Absolutely not! God's grace is not a license to sin and mistreat others, and neither is love.

WHAT AGAPE LOVE DOES

Verse 6 (continued):
"...but rejoices with the truth."

An atmosphere of genuine agape love is the perfect space for honest and open communication. A person won't fear admitting a failure or fault to a parent, relative, spouse or friend when they know the response will be love instead of judgment or condemnation. To know that their child feels safe enough and trusts them enough to share in this manner is any parent's joy. In the same manner, God is pleased when we admit our faults and tell Him the truth.

LOVE CHECK – The Love Chapter: 1 Corinthians 13

<u>Love celebrates the truth</u> rather than a lie. It's no fun finding out that someone has lied to you or done something bad, especially if the damages from those actions are great or potentially great. However, if a person is truthful and up front about what they've done (rather than only admitting the truth after being caught or being exposed later without confession), the responses and reactions may be much different. Those who are rewarded for doing wrong tend to continue in that vein or become unruly, disrespectful, bratty, spoiled and bad mannered over time. On the contrary, those who are rewarded for doing good and telling the truth, even when the truth may not always be pleasant, the opposite may occur. Again, whatever you praise and reward is magnified. So why not encourage good behavior and truthfulness?

LOVE CHECK – The Love Chapter: 1 Corinthians 13

Verse 7:

"Love bears all things, believes all things, hopes all things, endures all things."

Listen, as you can probably see by now, love is not for the faint of heart or for the weak. Verse 7 starts with one of the toughest things that love does – love <u>bears all things</u>. Whew! Let's unpack that a little. To bear something is to carry the weight of it – all the baggage, the drama, the moods, the difficulties,

"Because we have the God-given capacity to bear whatever God allows, love then is the vehicle. Wear love like a backpack."

the behaviors that come along with a person. It persists and perseveres through all hardships and challenges. Another Bible translation (the ERV, Easy-to-Read Version) says verse 7 like this: "Love never gives up on people. It never stops trusting, never loses hope, and never quits." It's this aspect of love that allows us to forgive, to believe in and love on someone

LOVE CHECK – The Love Chapter: 1 Corinthians 13

even if they've disappointed or hurt us, and to give someone another chance even if logic says they don't deserve it. This is the picture of God's heart toward us – knowing we will fail Him daily, yet loving us without the slightest drop in intensity or intentionality.

The good thing is that God has promised that He will never put more on us than we can bear. So because we have the God-given capacity to bear whatever God allows, love then is the vehicle. Wear love like a backpack.

That being said, in situations involving abuse and violence of any kind, we must protect and remove ourselves for our own survival and sanity. Since God loves us with such intensity and tender, loving care, surely He doesn't approve of anyone doing us physical, emotional or sexual harm.

LOVE CHECK – The Love Chapter: 1 Corinthians 13

To say that love <u>believes all things</u> is to say in essence that love chooses to see the good in the present, to give people the benefit of the doubt, believing that God is working in them just like He's working in us and that He will complete what He started in them. Love believes that no one is a lost cause, a failure, incapable of redemption, or unworthy of love. Love looks for and thus sees the best in people. God sees us as His perfect creation, the person that we are becoming, and the object of His affection. To love is to see through the eyes of God. It's been said that love is blind. In actuality, real love **sees** the good and the bad, but chooses to look beyond the flaws and faults it sees.

> *"Love looks for and thus sees the best in people… To love is to see through the eyes of God."*

To <u>hope all things</u> is to look on the bright side, **expecting** only the best from and for that loved one, and esteeming them worthy of all the best that life has to offer. Almost identical to believing all things, hoping all things is more future focused. Our outlook is always a positive one in regard to those we love. No matter what happens or what state they are in, our faith and trust in God makes us hopeful that God has great things in store for them and He's not done with them yet.

Love <u>endures all things</u> means that love can go the distance. A typical 15-round boxing match can leave a boxer weary, to say the least, and some don't make it to the final round. But whatever punches are thrown in *life*, at the end of the day and the end of each round, love is still standing. Love can take it. Love fights with words of affirmation, warm affection, acts of kindness, humble service, gentleness, patience, encouragement, courage under fire, etc, all those lovely things that bring joy, light and life to another being. Love is a worthy opponent, even stronger than death.

LOVE CHECK – The Love Chapter: 1 Corinthians 13

Verse 8:

"Love never ends. As for prophecies, they will pass away; as for tongues, they will cease; as for knowledge, it will pass away."

Real love is eternal, everlasting, and <u>never ends</u>. The nature of a relationship or how love is expressed may change, but love remains. People may physically and emotionally move on, divorce and remarry, or eventually learn to love someone else. But if you've ever truly loved someone, you always will. If someone says to you, "I don't love you anymore" and means it, trust; they never really did. Love doesn't work like that. You can't flip a switch in hopes that it will go off. You can't wish it away or numb it away. You can't shake it off or block it out. Time won't even erase it. Love is a powerful force that lives

"A world where there is more love than not is a better world."

LOVE CHECK – The Love Chapter: 1 Corinthians 13

forever. So beware that love bug; once bitten, it's got you. But that's a good thing. *A world where there is more love than not is a better world.* Many things may come to an end – prophecies, tongues, knowledge, etc. – but love isn't one of them.

Verses 9 thru 12:

"For we know in part and we prophesy in part, 10 but when the perfect comes, the partial will pass away. 11 When I was a child, I spoke like a child, I thought like a child, I reasoned like a child. When I became a man, I gave up childish ways. 12 For now we see in a mirror dimly, but then face to face. Now I know in part; then I shall know fully, even as I have been fully known."

In this world, we can only see a mere glimpse of who God is. God is love in its most perfect form. He fully knows us (the good and the bad), and He loves us still. As we are matured and perfected by love, it strengthens and grows and gradually reveals the truth of who God is. One day we will come to know Him fully, as we see Him in all His glory.

Verse 13:

"So now faith, hope, and love abide, these three; but the greatest of these is love."

Strip away the superficial layers of life, down to the bare bones, and you'll see what's truly important, what's really at the foundation of it all. Though faith can move mountains and hope survives in the direst of situations; hands down, love is the greatest power in the world, for God is Love.

LOVE CHECK – The Love Chapter: 1 Corinthians 13

<u>1 CORINTHIANS 13 LOVE TEST:</u>

To give yourself or someone else a quick "love check," try this on for size. Put your name or their name in the empty spaces. If the paragraph is true with that name there, congrats, you/they passed the test! If not, there's more internal work to do (please review this chapter and the resources at the end of this book).

_____ is patient and kind; _____ does not envy or boast; _____ is not arrogant or rude. _____ does not insist on [his/her] own way; _____ is not irritable or resentful; _____ does not rejoice at wrongdoing, but rejoices with the truth. _____ bears all things, believes all things, hopes all things, endures all things. _____'s love never ends.

CHAPTER 4

JESUS: THE BLUEPRINT

> *"...With both feet planted firmly on love, you'll be able to take in with all followers of Jesus the extravagant dimensions of Christ's love. Reach out and experience the breadth! Test its length! Plumb the depths! Rise to the heights! Live full lives, full in the fullness of God."*
>
> *~Ephesians 3:17-19 MSG*

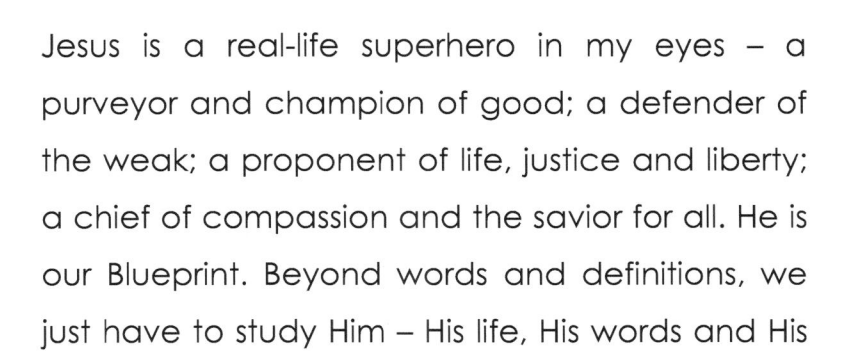

Jesus is a real-life superhero in my eyes – a purveyor and champion of good; a defender of the weak; a proponent of life, justice and liberty; a chief of compassion and the savior for all. He is our Blueprint. Beyond words and definitions, we just have to study Him – His life, His words and His deeds – to see love personified. He *is* Love, in essence and in action. The following tidbits are archived posts from one of my social media pages, describing Jesus as the perfect example for how we should conduct ourselves in love (*feel free to post, tweet or share these powerful truths on your pages with hashtag #lovecheck*):

As you go through the 4 gospels, you see the amazing character, love and nature of #Jesus. Constantly in awe of Him. Who wouldn't serve a God like this?

Every act of #Jesus was a lesson, usually in #Love. Study Him. Know Him. #4Gospels #Matthew #Mark #Luke #John

If I had to describe #Jesus in one word, it would have to be #Love. That was the signature and brand of His entire ministry. #4Gospels #KnowHim

LOVE CHECK – Jesus: The Blueprint

Let's explore these truths about Jesus a little further, as we delve into the 4 Gospels.

Each of the gospels (Matthew, Mark, Luke & John) is loaded with examples of Jesus' love in action. In this chapter, only key passages are mentioned. They are grouped together for easier exploration like so: 1) Love That Sees, 2) Love That Serves, 3) Love That Honors, 4) Love That Empathizes, 5) Love That Teaches & Demonstrates, 6) Labor Of Love, 7) Tough Love, and 8) Sacrificial Love. In your own spare time, I encourage you to read the noted verses, in addition to the following summaries, that highlight who Jesus really is.

1. LOVE THAT SEES
"What is it He sees in me?"

Love doesn't choose people according to typical societal standards of prestige, beauty, grandeur, popularity, stature, etc. He often chooses the unlikely, the ordinary, the unknown, the overlooked, the outcast and the marginalized in society. He looks beyond the surface and looks directly into the heart. He recognizes all their God-given potential, because He put it there.

Those whom man would deem as unworthy or unfit to be the conduit and bloodline through which their Son/a King would be born, God chose as Jesus' ancestral predecessors: Rahab the prostitute (**Matthew 1:5**); as well as King David and wise King Solomon (**Matthew 1:6**), both of whom were notoriously known for their failings with women. Jesus' own mother was an obscure, young woman born in an obscure town (**Luke 1:26-33**). The first disciples Jesus chose to help expand His ministry were ordinary people with flaws (**Mark 1:17**). For example, Peter was a hot-tempered fisherman

"It doesn't matter if you're standing alone or in the midst of a crowd, Love sees you right where you are."

and Matthew was a tax collector, unwelcome amongst his people. Jesus fellowshipped and spent time with the Matthews of the Bible, those who were considered outcasts or sinners, to show that they too were worthy of His love (**Matthew 9:9-13**).

It doesn't matter if you're standing alone or in the midst of a crowd, Love sees you right where you are. Case in point, the woman who suffered with an issue of blood for 12 years: On the way to heal someone else, Jesus stops and heals this woman, because she had pressed her way through to reach Him in the midst of a crowd. This was a woman who society had overlooked and labeled unclean. It was her faith that got His attention, but Love *saw* her right in the midst of her affliction when others couldn't or wouldn't see (**Luke 8:43-48**). Oh, how He loves you!

2. LOVE THAT SERVES

"Why is He serving me when I should be serving Him?"

Philippians 2:6-9 describes Jesus perfectly as the epitome of humility, a perfect image of what it means to truly have a servant's heart:

"...Though He was in the form of God, did not count equality with God a thing to be grasped, but emptied Himself, by taking the form of a servant, being born in the likeness of men. And being found in human form, He humbled Himself by becoming obedient to the point of death, even death on a cross. Therefore God has highly exalted Him and bestowed on Him the name that is above every name."

Jesus was even born in humble conditions, in a manger (**Luke 2:7**), and heralded as King upon His entry into Jerusalem on a **donkey** – not how you might expect a King to make his grand

LOVE CHECK – Jesus: The Blueprint

entrance (**Matthew 21:1-11**). He often kept a low profile and consorted with people from all walks of life, especially the poor and the afflicted.

In **John 5:3-11**, Jesus teaches the Beatitudes, which give special encouragement and honor to those who typically followed Him – the poor, the hungry, the thirsty, the disheartened, the humble, the peacemakers and the persecuted. These are those society tends to disregard, yet Jesus took time to minister to them. A King who serves His subjects – what a beautiful image of love!

In this posture, Jesus was more down-to-earth and approachable. The spirit in which He served others made His love more tangible and impactful. Jesus had no problem submitting to or serving both someone in authority and someone who was technically His subordinate. It greatly pleased God

"A King who serves His subjects – what a beautiful image of love!"

the Father, for example, when Jesus submitted Himself to His cousin, John the Baptist's authority and let John baptize Him in the Jordan River (**Luke 3:21-22**).

In **Mark 10:45**, Jesus makes it clear that He came into the world not to be served, but to serve and to give His life for mankind's salvation. Who could forget how on the night of the Last Supper before He died, Jesus served His disciples by washing **their** feet (**John 13:4-5**)! You might think, Shouldn't that be the other way around? Shouldn't they be washing **His** feet? It was a lesson in humility, servitude and honor. Jesus wanted them to follow His example as their leader, serving both those under His authority and those who worked alongside Him. (**John 13:12-17**).

> *"If you serve all people, despite their status or rank, there's no room for discrimination or inequality."*

To me, this further reinforces the fact that Jesus was not a respecter of persons. If you serve all people, despite their status or rank, there's no room for discrimination or inequality. Serving those less fortunate or those under our authority automatically keeps us in a posture of humility. If people are always singing your praises, it could go to your head and manifest itself as arrogance and pride; and with so much focus on self, consequently, love suffers. See how that works? Even the smallest lessons that Jesus taught were deeply profound.

Something else amazing happens when we are serving others: It brings joy to both us and those we're serving. You may find that you're happier or happiest when you're giving, serving and pouring into others. Don't be stingy in your giving and servitude if you want to be abundantly blessed in this way. Love will reward you!

3. LOVE THAT HONORS
"Am I worthy?"

Love is no respecter of persons, plain and simple. He doesn't esteem one person higher than another based on the superficial. Jesus was a heart reader. It didn't matter if you were an ordinary citizen or a Roman official; He received and honored the request of anyone who humbly came to Him in faith.

In **Matthew 8:5-13**, for example, Jesus grants the request of a Roman soldier to heal his paralyzed servant and honors him because of His great faith, even though Roman soldiers were generally unwelcome among His people. In **Matthew 15:21-28**, Jesus honors the faith of a persistent Canaanite woman who begs Him to heal her demon-possessed daughter, even though He wasn't called to her people. In **John 4:7-29**, Jesus engages in conversation with and gives divine revelation to a

Samaritan woman, who is considered unwelcome among the Jewish people.

In **Mark 10:14-15**, Jesus even welcomes little children into His space, giving them special honor, though His disciples and others shunned them. Jesus says that those who would enter His kingdom must be humble and meek like little children.

"Jesus made a promise: 'Whoever comes to Me, I will never cast out."

No matter who you are or where you come from, Jesus made a promise "...whoever comes to Me, I will never cast out" (**John 6:37**). Oh, how He loves you!

4. LOVE THAT EMPATHIZES

"Does He really care about me and my situation?"

The heart of God is tender and His love truly limitless toward humanity. According to Hebrews 1:3, Jesus is the "exact imprint of His nature." Because Jesus got to experience firsthand what it's like to walk the earth and live as a human being among us, He can truly relate to the emotions, temptations, thoughts and circumstances we deal with from day to day. Hebrews 4:15 says, "…we do not have a high priest who is unable to sympathize with our weaknesses," because quite literally He's been there. Though faith is something that definitely gets His attention, Love is also touched by our pain and our plight. He wants to see us free, healed and whole – physically, mentally and spiritually.

Have you ever found yourself in a situation where you needed God's help or healing, and you've been waiting a long time, but still haven't gotten what you were seeking? Jesus encountered such a man in **John 5:2-9**, who had been paralyzed or crippled for 38 years. Jesus found Him by the pool of Bethesda (which means "House of Mercy" or

"House of Grace" in Hebrew) and realized that He had been there for a long time. Love had compassion. Love sought him out. Love was determined not to leave him the way He found him. The crippled man was sitting right in a place of healing but couldn't seem to get healed. Jesus asks Him if He even **wanted** to be healed; it was a question of faith. How bad did he really want it? The man began to explain his plight and how every time He would try to get into the healing waters, someone would always beat him to it. Hearing this, Jesus simply commanded the man to get up, take up his mat and walk. Jesus was making it clear that faith has no limitations, and that He, Himself, was the Healer. Needless to say, that was the last day that man spent crippled; Love healed him, but it was his faith and obedience that sealed the deal.

In **John, chapter 9**, Jesus encounters a beggar, who daily sat in darkness, being blind from birth. But how could darkness encounter Light and not be changed? The immediate assumption upon seeing his plight, by men, was that his blindness was a result of either his or his parent's sins (**John 9:6-7**). Jesus knew better; in actuality, the man's blindness was allowed so that his healing would show forth the works of God. The ironic thing is that after Jesus heals the man, Jewish leaders accuse both him and Jesus of being sinners – Jesus, for healing him on the Sabbath and him, for supposedly "faking his blindness" and attributing his sight to Jesus. They consequently threw him out of the temple. The audacity! Could it be that sometimes people prefer to see you broken rather than healed, needy rather than full, bound rather than free, in darkness rather than light? "Church hurt" was a thing even in the Bible days. But at the moment they spurned him, Love embraced him.

"'Church hurt' was a thing even in the Bible days."

Not enough can be said about the level of mercy and compassion that Jesus has for His people. In **John 8:7-11**, Jesus defends a woman caught in adultery against her accusers, and saves her from being stoned. He sends her away restored, with the firm, but simple command to sin no more. Love chooses to cover rather than expose, to forgive rather than condemn.

In similar fashion, in **Luke 7:36-50**, Jesus defends a fallen woman against those who criticized her for kneeling and weeping at His feet, using expensive oil to anoint His feet and drying them with her hair. They couldn't see past her sins and her radical act in the house of a dignitary. Hers was an act of worship, humility and love, and Jesus honored her for it. In the midst of rejection, Love accepted her. He forgave her for the many sins she had committed and sent her on her way in peace.

The shortest verse in the Bible highlights Jesus' love for His friends, just prior to Him performing one of the greatest miracles recorded in Bible history. **John 11:35** is only two words: "Jesus wept." He was moved to tears at the news of His friend Lazarus' death and upon witnessing the sorrow of Lazarus's sisters. **John 11:38-44** describes the awesome moments when Jesus raised Lazarus from the dead. In any dead or seemingly impossible situation, it's important to remember that Love is the Resurrection and the Life. Oh, how He loves you!

5. LOVE THAT TEACHES & DEMONSTRATES

"Does His presence in my life make me or my life better?"

Jesus made it a habit of imparting wisdom, teaching and preaching wherever He went to whoever would listen. You see, an encounter with Love won't leave you the way you were before. Love wants to see you better off. Love wants to eradicate ignorance and help you increase in

"Love wants to see you better off... love doesn't just tell you; love shows you."

knowledge and truth. Love wants to introduce you to new ways of thinking, new ways of seeing, and new ways of being that perhaps you hadn't considered. Love doesn't just tell you; love shows you. Love unlocks the confines of your mind and heart, and opens you up to a world of better and more.

Have you ever failed a test, but no one explained to you why? Like, how can you pass the next time or how can you improve if you don't know where you missed the mark? Jesus' disciples had seen Him heal countless numbers of people on many occasions, yet in one instance they found themselves unable to do what they had seen Him do. In addition to a rebuke, it was a teaching moment. So rather than leave them at the point of bewilderment on what they might've done wrong, Jesus performs the healing, and then explains why they didn't succeed. Not only was it due to their unbelief, but fasting and prayer were also required **(Matthew 17:14-21)**,

We could also revisit **John 13**, where Jesus teaches His disciples by example what servitude and humility looks like, as He washes their feet. See, not only did He do it; He explained why. And His explanation reinforced the fact that contrary to popular belief, in God's Kingdom, greatness is measured quite differently. Child-like humility is the indication and requirement of greatness (**Matthew 18:1-4**), and those who aspire to be great must be the greatest servant (**Matthew 20:20-28**).

In the Sermon on the Mount (**Matthew 5**), Jesus breaks down all kinds of spiritual truths, providing clarity and expounding on teachings of old with new revelation. In verses **39-44**, He teaches that if we are to walk in love, we should resist the urge for revenge; we should give freely, even to those who try to steal from us; we should go the extra mile when asked to do something; we should give to those in need; and we should love our enemies, just to name a few. And you best believe He practiced what He preached, always leading by example.

In **Matthew 6:9-13**, Jesus even takes time to teach His disciples how to pray effectively, and then spends the entirety of **John, chapter 17**, praying fervently for them.

Jesus taught and demonstrated that God is the unlimited Source for whatever we need. In **Matthew 7:7-11**, Jesus reminds us that God loves to give good things to His children, if they will only ask and seek after them. **John 4:10,13-14** declares Jesus to be a wellspring of life and abundance. Jesus turns little into much in **Luke 6:9-14** when He feeds a crowd of over 5,000 people and in **John 2:1-11** when, at His mother's request, He turns water into an overflow of fine wine.

In **Mark 12:33**, Jesus condenses the original 10 commandments into two primary commandments (which still embody them all) to make it easier for His disciples to understand and do them – love

God supremely and love your neighbor as yourself. In **Matthew 25:31-46**, Jesus places great value on our love and care for one another – especially the least among us – which He counts as service to Him. He declares that only those who love Him and others in this manner will be found worthy to go to heaven. Daily, they witnessed Him putting this love into practice, by how He treated them and others, but chiefly how He honored and obeyed God. Oh, how He loves you!

6. LABOR OF LOVE
"Will He ever grow tired of me?"

Selflessly and tirelessly, Jesus labored in love. The 4 gospels document how He traveled from place to place, teaching, preaching and healing the masses. Wherever He went, the crowds followed, barely allowing Him a moment's rest, yet He took the time to faithfully and diligently minister during moments of inconvenience, grief, fatigue, anger, etc. His compassion and love for the people drove Him to put their needs above His own.

In **Matthew 14:13-14**, for example, even though the crowds followed Him, barely allowing Him a moment alone to pray and to mourn John the Baptist's death, Jesus was moved with compassion when He saw them, and healed them anyway.

Mark 1:32-39 is another prime example of the great demand on Jesus' life. In this passage, Jesus had spent all evening ministering, as large crowds thronged Him at the door of the home He was in. He rose early the next morning to find a quiet place to pray, but was still searched out by His disciples because the crowds were steadily asking for Him. With limited rest and time to recharge, Love pressed through for the sake of the people, **continuing** to preach, teach and minister.

In **John 5:16-17**, when Jewish leaders scold Jesus for healing a crippled man on the Sabbath, against

Jewish law; Jesus acknowledges that He will work, like His Father, even on the Sabbath – if someone needs to be healed. When Jewish leaders scold Him for healing a blind man on the Sabbath in **John, chapter 9**, clearly they were more concerned with downplaying and diminishing the miracle of healing by casting doubt and highlighting the law. Love was more concerned with seeing a man made whole. Jesus is clearly operating in love in both instances, thus fulfilling the law. Oh, how He loves you!

7. TOUGH LOVE
"Can He handle my mistakes?"

Everyone enjoys the beautiful and tender aspects of love – the kindness, affection, service, endearing words, etc. But no one likes the flip side of love – the kind of love that rebukes, chastises and corrects. Nevertheless, there is beauty in tough love, too. It's often a swift, firm and sometimes aggressive move that will curb us from danger and destruction. We might never recognize our faults and mistakes otherwise. We might never see that we're headed in the wrong direction or toward danger unless someone or something intervenes in, what seems at the time to be, an unpleasant manner. Think of the child you might have to suddenly snatch back and away from a hot stove so they won't get burned, or the stranger you have to push out of the way of an oncoming car to save their life. The sensation of being aggressively and suddenly yanked or pushed in these instances may be shocking and even painful to the child or the stranger; but once they realize that it was necessary to save them from pain or death, they can understand. Now, they get it. Having to temporarily feel a little pain or discomfort is better than having to experience the excruciating and possible long-term effects of what might have been.

"It's often a swift, firm and sometimes aggressive move that will curb us from danger and destruction."

Jesus was a radical and a revolutionary when He had to be, and He was no stranger to tough love. He knew that souls and lives were at stake, and so He taught and acted in ways that sometimes provoked the Jewish leaders and people of His day. His intent, however, was to transform their thinking, get them to see the error of their ways, change the course of their lives for the better and give them a chance at eternal life.

In **Mark 2:13-17**, Jesus is going on what appeared to be a rampage to cleanse the temple in Jerusalem – turning over tables, berating and driving out the money-changers who He believed were defiling the house of God. The temple was sacred and holy, a place of prayer and worship, not a marketplace. With this act, Jesus was also teaching people the importance of having reverence and love for God and God's house.

LOVE CHECK – Jesus: The Blueprint

In **Matthew 15:1-20**, even though the Pharisees are offended by the truth He teaches, Jesus continues to do so for their own good and that of others listening. He wasn't afraid to call them out, nor was He afraid to defend Himself or His disciples when they accused them falsely. Jesus continues to go on a tirade, rebuking the Pharisees', Sadducees' and scribes' hypocrisy and error pertaining to religious laws and traditions. But by **Matthew 23:37**, He pours out His heart, lamenting over His people and reminding them of the many times He's wanted to embrace them like a mother hen protects Her chickens, but they wouldn't receive Him nor His messengers sent before Him.

In **Matthew 16:21-23**, Peter probably got the shock of his life when Jesus berated him for trying to convince Jesus that He wouldn't have to suffer persecution and death in Jerusalem. Peter was essentially stating that Jesus wouldn't fulfill His prophetic mission that He came to earth for, setting Himself in opposition to God's will. Jesus quickly retorted: "Get behind me, Satan! You are a hindrance to Me." Even this rebuke was an act of love, because it was meant to correct Peter, and adjust his attitude and thinking in alignment with God.

In **Matthew 17:22-23**, Jesus, known to speak the truth even at inconvenient times, because He'd rather people be prepared than comfortable, again warns His disciples of His soon-coming death and resurrection. In **Matthew 24**, Jesus warns His disciples of the terrifying signs of the end of the world, so that they and/or their descendants could be prepared and not left behind when it occurs. He loved them enough to tell them the truth.

In **John 18:10**, Jesus rebukes Peter for violently defending Him against the soldiers who came to arrest Him, seeking to not only spare Peter's life but also because He knew He must be obedient to God's will for His life. And because of His steadfast obedience, we have the free gift of salvation available to us today. Oh, how He loves you!

8. SACRIFICIAL LOVE
"What price would He pay for me?"

Jesus' life was marked by sacrifice, but no doubt, His greatest sacrifice was His willingness and obedience to follow His intended mission, for the sake of humanity, all the way to the cross. In **Matthew 26:39, 42**, we can plainly see Jesus' internal struggle with His decision. He wrestled with the idea of having to die a painful death on the cross, as He prayed to His Father in the Garden of Gethsemane. He humbly surrendered to the will of God anyway out of obedience and love for mankind.

And when it was time to face judgment before His sentencing and death, Jesus was a trooper. In the face of all kinds of accusations against Him,

Jesus remains silent (**Matthew 27:14**), and chooses not to fight back when spit on, mocked and struck by Jewish leaders (**Matthew 26:67-68**). Jesus was handed over and given a death sentence by the very ones who only a few days prior welcomed, celebrated and worshipped Him, many to whom He had also ministered and healed.

Jesus was an innocent man, viciously beaten, nailed to the cross and placed between two thieves like a common criminal (**Matthew 27:26, 38**). Yet, in **Luke 23:34**, Jesus goes so far as to pray for those who were persecuting Him, asking God to forgive them for being ignorant of what they were doing. What kind of love would lead a man to intercede for the very ones persecuting and abusing Him – at the very point of death?!

"Love refused to come down from the cross to save His own life. He was committed to completing His mission."

Feeling excruciating pain and utter humiliation, facing the fear of certain death, feeling alone and abandoned by His Father in His darkest hour, still love kept Him on that cross. Love refused to come down from the cross to save His own life (**Matthew 27:42-46**). He was committed to completing His mission. He "endured the cross, despising the shame" (Hebrews 12:2), because He was focused on the joy and the victory that lie ahead. This was the price He was willing to pay for the sins of all of humanity. Oh, how He loves you!

CHAPTER 5

MR. & MRS. RIGHT?

> *"Love is like a friendship caught on fire. In the beginning a flame, very pretty, often hot and fierce, but still only light and flickering. As love grows older, our hearts mature and our love becomes as coals, deep-burning and unquenchable."*
>
> *~Bruce Lee*

I hate to see marriages and relationships fail – especially really good ones. Couples you've seen really happy and fulfilled at one point in time (at least from our perspective) and then somehow things turn sour. I'm sure many of us can relate. The Bible even says that God hates divorce. I've heard people describe divorce like being ripped apart, and I would imagine that's exactly how it feels when you start out as two individuals and friends (the **philos** type of love), evolve into becoming one, and then have to split all over again. Catch *that* visual. What God joins together, no man (woman, boy, or girl) should tear it apart.

A Pearl of Great Price

Jesus mentions in Matthew 13:45-46 a parable, or story, about a merchant in search of fine pearls. When he sets his eyes on **thee** finest pearl he had ever seen, the merchant goes and sells all he has to obtain it. Though Jesus was referring to the kingdom of heaven in this illustration, I'd like to think of this as a beautiful parallel to what it's like finding the perfect mate that God has ordained for you. You'd give practically anything for it. It's worth it. Worth the wait. Worth the search. Worth the price.

LOVE CHECK – Mr. & Mrs. Right?

If you're waiting for Mr. Right or searching for Mrs. Right, the same principles and truths on love already discussed in this book can still apply. But hey, we're all different; so there's nothing wrong with knowing what you like and dislike, and having your own list of qualities and characteristics you desire in a mate. Sis might be jotting down, "He's gotta be tall, dark and handsome, hardworking, witty and kind, faithful and intelligent…" Bro might be saying, "She's gotta be fit and fine, friendly, caring and kind, smart, cool and down to earth…" Listen, to each his/her own. But if it's **real love** you're seeking or checking for, "The Love Chapter" can definitely serve as a measuring stick or guide – even when it comes to a current and/or potential mate. None of us is exempt from God's Metric System; and though agape love is all-encompassing, marriage and romantic relationships also open us up to a world of passion and desire, and introduce the type of love known as **Eros**. This is the attraction factor, the romantic, sensual and physical side of love shared between couples – and it's okay. God created this aspect of love, too, as part of the enjoyment of covenant and building of family. No other home is as strong or as beautiful as the one Love built.

So though our #1 Source and our primary Teacher is God when it comes to love, another reliable source of insight is a couple that has been successful in marriage for the long term – those who have stood the test of time, who are truly happy and enjoying being together, who have plenty of great and lasting memories, and even some tears to prove it. I'm talking 20, 30, 40 and 50+ years of marriage. These are the proverbial "love doctors" among us, who can tell us a thing or two about what it takes to walk in love, hand in hand.

Wisdom about love can only come from God, experience and proven insight from those who have walked the walk and talked the talk. Here's some wisdom for the ages... Take a peek into the heart of three beautiful couples and discover what made them Mr. and Mrs. Right.

A Candid Look At Love: The Interviews

These interviews were conducted virtually or electronically AFTER the rest of the book was written. They are transcribed and abridged for this book. This was actually the last portion added. Yet, I was surprised to see that many of their answers line up with what I believe about marriage and what it takes to sustain it. That is really encouraging. I was truly blessed by these interviews and testimonies, because what it did was prove very clearly and candidly (for anyone who still doubts) that the agape love described in 1 Corinthians 13 works; that the bar that seems to be set so high there is attainable; that it **is** possible for individuals to achieve and it **is** possible within the confines of marriage. Their stories are awe-inspiring, thought-provoking and real. So sit back, get your favorite snack or drink (don't mind my theatrics), and take a peak into the window of what real love looks like, as told from the perspective of lovebirds who have 20+ years of marriage under their belt. We can learn a lot from them. Hearts open.

Maurice & Sherita Wilson (20 Years)
"GOD ASKED ME IF I COULD LOVE HIM... I SAID 'YES...'"

Q: How would you define love? Does it look different in a marriage?

Maurice: Love is responsibility, a sacrifice, a death to your will and what you think is right. It's an action. It's work, as opposed to something that you feel. Real love has a whole lot less to do with feelings than most people think. God is love. He loved us so much that He became our sacrifice. Love looks differently in marriage. Before you're married, you love the way you think you should love. But once you come into covenant, you have to love your wife the way God loves her. You take on that responsibility.

You become the sacrifice – placing her needs above your own.

Sherita: Someone once said, "Love is as love does." Others say, "It's not a feeling, but an action." I define love as a choice. It is a choice that has to be made every day. Every day we get to choose to love each other. And hopefully, with that choice, we choose to love each other better than the day before. For me, love definitely looks different in a marriage. For one, as long as we were just dating, I knew I still had the option of walking away. So did my husband. However, once we married, the rules changed. First, our lives had become intertwined. So, walking away meant we'd have to unravel our finances, housing situation, and most importantly the lives of our children. Then there's the promise I made my husband to love him for better or worse, for richer or poorer, and in sickness and in health. Walking away would have reduced my vow to mere words. Finally, I made God a promise.

One day as my mother and I were walking to the neighborhood grocery store, I saw my husband across the street. I knew him from our church choir, but that was all I knew about him. In that moment, God asked me if I could love him. I said, "Yes. If he's a good man and if he's understanding, then yes, I can love him." We would be married before I remembered having that encounter with God. Every argument or life situation since then that has made me want to walk away has brought me back to that hill where I had that exchange with God. God asked me if I could love him and I said yes. To walk away and leave him when he's down, broken and imperfect would make my vow to God null and void, my vow to my husband null and void and would totally interrupt and unravel the lives of our children. There is

"Failure is not an option. Because 1 Corinthians 13 says Love never fails."

another level of commitment and strength that is applied to love once you are married. Failure is not an option. Because 1 Corinthians 13 says Love never fails.

Q: Going back to the beginning of your marriage (becoming one, learning to live in harmony), what did love look like? How has this evolved throughout your marriage?

Maurice: In the beginning, our love was immature – like freshly planted seeds. But over the years, it has been cultivated and it has blossomed into a garden. It's been fertilized, tilled, and tried. It's so much richer now because it has been worked. I thought I knew what love was when I got married. But I had no idea how much deeper, fuller, richer, and just brighter it could be by just working at it. All of my preconceptions about love before I got married have been challenged and proven to be immature. Since then, I have come to realize you only get out of a thing what you put into it. Love can grow, but you have to work at it.

Sherita: Like most marriages, our marriage enjoyed its honeymoon years. In those years, neither of us really could do any wrong. Even when we were wrong, it was overlooked for the sake of love. And so, the honeymoon, or fairytale, continued. However, as we approach our 20th anniversary, I've come to understand that there is a responsibility in love. If I love my husband, it is my responsibility to see that he becomes everything God is calling him to be. And vice versa. Sometimes, that means you can't overlook what you see. Instead, you have to address it if you are ever going to overcome it. I used to say all the time, "You have to call it out before you can cast it out." So, we've learned to call some things out in our marriage. Whether they were bad habits or stinking thinking. Then we worked together to

"Love doesn't mean overlook, it means overcome!"

cast them out of our marriage. And it might not look like it, but this act of sharpening each other is also love. I love him enough to address anything I see in him, on him or around him that does not reflect my love for him or his divinity in God. In short, we've learned that love doesn't mean overlook, it means overcome!

Q: Can you remember how you viewed love as a child? What would you tell your 16-year-old selves about what it means to ENDURE in love?

Maurice: Growing up in a single-parent household, for me love is being there, and not being there is not love. I'm not sure I spent a lot of time thinking about love as a youth. I was loved by my grandmother, who was there for me. I was loved by my mother, who was there for me. Anyone who wasn't there for me didn't love me. That's

"Love is not what's depicted on TV. It's not a feeling in your stomach or music in your head..."

how you think as a child. It's pretty black and white. I would tell my 16-year-old self that love is not what's depicted on TV. It's not a feeling in the pit of your stomach, or music playing in your head. I would tell myself what the Bible says about love. Love is patient and kind. Before I tried to tell myself how to endure in it, I would want to properly introduce myself to who Love is.

Sherita: As a child, I viewed love through the eyes of my mother. I remember walking to Eastover Shopping Center with my mother when I was about seven years old. I remember looking up at her and saying, "I know I'm a big disappointment to you." At the time, I remember feeling really small. I think I may have even begun to cry. My mother stopped me in my tracks and told me how she could never be disappointed in me and how much she loved me and would always love me. As we continued our walk, I began to skip. My mother loved me, and she would love me no matter what. By the time I was 16, there were a lot of "no matter what's." Only now, there was no time for reassurance. Life was in full gear and everybody had to pull their weight. Going without that reassurance left me feeling unloved. I didn't understand at the time how hard the life was my mother was choosing to live for me and my siblings. As a single parent, she had to do everything herself. I wish I could tell my 16-year-old self that love goes beyond words. It's getting up early in the morning and facing the bitter cold to go to a job you hate because your kids need a roof over their heads, clothes on their backs, shoes for their feet and food in their bellies. Love chooses to stay in the fight even when the cost to oneself seems too steep to ever recover. The Bible says it this way: Love bears all things, believes all things, hopes for all things, and endures all things. Love never fails.

> *"Love chooses to stay in the fight even when the cost to oneself seems too steep…"*

Q: Why do you think God says in 1 Corinthians 13 that love is the greatest between hope, faith, and love?

Maurice: I think it's because having love is equivalent to having God. Everything else will come and go. Hope will come and go. Faith will come and go. But having love, love is that lasting element that you need. Love became flesh and bore our sins. It was lied on, ridiculed, despised, and rejected. Those are just some of the things love endured. If I could choose to have only one of these in my life, I would rather have love. For God is love.

> *"Having love is equivalent to having God. Everything else will come and go..."*

Sherita: The Bible ever only equates God to one of these three things. It does not say God is hope. It does not say God is faith. But it does say in 1 John 4:8, God is love.

LOVE CHECK – Mr. & Mrs. Right?

Q: After taking a closer look at 1 Corinthians 13, if you were to insert your spouse's name into the text, how would you both measure up?

Maurice: I think my wife exemplifies the text in 1 Corinthians 13. I think she can do this because she knows God. The closer she gets to God, the more His love is poured out through her. For myself, as I get closer to God, I can insert myself more and more into these passages. I might be a little closer with some of the scriptures than others. But I feel the closer the walk, the closer the reflection. You see less of me and more of Him.

Sherita: If you look at the text in the Message version, it says Love doesn't keep score of the sins of others. Unfortunately, the way my mind works...I'm a score keeper. I can tell you who did what, when, how many times, what they were wearing, where we were standing, what I was thinking, how it made me feel...the list goes on. I don't think I'm this way maliciously. There are just some pivotal moments in a relationship where what's being said or done makes a lasting impression. There are times when prayer and forgiveness aren't instantaneous for me. Instead, it's a process that takes time. So there, my secret is out. I don't love perfectly. None of us love perfectly. Only God loves perfectly because He is a perfect God.

Now, Mr. Wilson, he is the reflection of God's love in my life. If there was ever an example of a man who comes close to living 1 Corinthians 13 out perfectly, it would be him. Maurice never gives up on me. He cares more for others than for himself. He doesn't want what he doesn't have. He doesn't strut or have a swelled head. He doesn't force himself on others. He isn't always "Me first." He doesn't fly off the handle. He doesn't keep score of the sins of others. He doesn't revel when others grovel. He takes pleasure in the flowering of truth. He puts up with anything. He trusts God always. He always looks for the best. He never looks back but keeps going to the end. And with God, Maurice cannot fail!

Pastor Marvin & 1st Lady Terry Wilson (44 Years)
"WE DIDN'T AGREE ON EVERYTHING... WE AGREED TO GET THINGS DONE..."

Q: How did you know you had found Mr. or Mrs. Right?

Terry: I think I knew when I knew that he could put up with this foolishness that I was putting out.

> *"I may not agree with you, but I agree to be **with** you."*

Marvin: There were times when we didn't agree on everything, but we agreed to get things done. That's how I knew. You always need somebody you can talk to and not talk at. I may not agree with you, but I agree to be **with** you.

LOVE CHECK – Mr. & Mrs. Right?

Q: Does love look different in a marriage?

Terry: Absolutely. In marriage, it's a willingness to share oneself with another and still remain individual. In marriage, it calls for a LOT of sacrifice and willingness to allow time and space for each other to be who God created you to be.

Q: Going back to the beginning of your marriage when you were becoming one or learning to live in harmony, what did love look like?

Terry: In the early days of marriage, it was "How are we gonna make this work after being single and self-supporting?" And I had to ask myself, "How much of me can I give up?" In the early days, I relied more on

"In marriage, it calls for a LOT of sacrifice..."

myself than God, only to learn through fatal mistakes that one could never have a successful marriage unless God is the Head and that both people are in agreement to follow God's word.

Marvin: In the beginning, we had to learn how to share. You have to learn her. You have to know her. And knowing her doesn't mean just sexually, but it means to try to know her mentally, all of those things. You had to pick and choose your battles. Do I really need to have that? Is it really necessary for me to have the last word? You really start to learn more about yourself, because you find out very early on that we're really very selfish people. You have to gain knowledge, understanding, wisdom; and all of these things come together...

Q: Next question. Can you remember how you viewed love as a child? What would you tell your 16-year-old self about what it means to ENDURE in love?

Marvin: I could go back to my grandparents, both sides. We were always family oriented, but we would always see them engage with each other. They would hug each other in the presence of their children. Then my parents were very unselfish, so they gave each other gifts. They did what each other wanted to do. And that's how I began to learn. I recognized that, that was the enduring kind of love. That was the kind of love that, through it all, they stuck it out. And that's what I wanted. I could tell my 16-year-old self, "Keep going."

Terry: I agree with Marvin that I viewed love, as a child, through my family. That influenced me the most. Then I was the type of person that lived in a fantasy world, because I lived with television and comic books and love stories; and so those are the kinds of things that influenced me... you know, I thought love was being white, because in those days when I was coming up, television was white. The experiences were white, and so who didn't want a nice family sitting at the table? So those are the kinds of things that I associated with love.

At 16, when I probably came out of the fantasy world and I'm living in the real world about now, I would probably tell myself to know God first, and that way I would not make the mistake of lustful love. I definitely didn't know much about love at 16, but the experiences were what I thought was love... I would tell that 16-year-old to first be an individual and don't follow someone else's manipulation. I definitely would stay true to myself and follow my own dreams, and I definitely would take it slow.

Q: Next question. Why do you think God says in 1 Corinthians 13 that love is the greatest between hope, faith and love?

Terry: I think He says that, because I look at love as an umbrella. In an umbrella you have spokes all the way around, and the umbrella provides a covering and protection. If you look up, you see that God is love and He is the center of everything, Then basically everything comes back to that.

Marvin: It's like an instruction from God. This is what you need to have for all of these other gifts to work. If you really want it to be effective, God says, "This is the one you want. If you're gonna desire anything, this is the one you want – Love." That's the way I see it.

Q: How long have you all been married?

Terry: Forty-four. It's crazy. It's insane. It's insanity. (laughs)

Marvin: Let me tell you about all those years: It's one day a time, because if you're looking long distance, you would be like, "I done had enough of this. I done had enough of your BS." But what love does is, love says, "Walk with me. I'm here. I'm not running away. I'm not going out to get a smoke and never return. I made a promise." And that's how you get through the first year. And they talk about your anniversaries? Your anniversaries are celebrations of creating or having a year, without taking each other out (laughter)... But if you can't laugh at yourself, you're not gonna make any years. If you can't indulge someone else's ideas, you're not gonna make any years. There are some times, as I said earlier, you're not gonna agree. But I love you anyhow, so let's deal with today. You're hot with me right now? OK; this too will pass. And if you're holding it against me, you're the only one holding it, because I sure don't. Some points in 1 Corinthians 13 will cause you to self-examine. That's what gets you through them years. And it's not just getting through it; it's living. If it sounds as though I'm just enduring this, no. Our first couple of years in this house? You would've thought we had a club. We had fun, ok? We had fun. (laughter)

> *"Some points in 1 Corinthians 13 will cause you to self-examine. That's what gets you through them years."*

Q: OK, this is my final question, but it is the most important question: After taking a closer look at [1 Corinthians 13], if you were to insert your spouse's name [in place of the word "love"], do they measure up and do you measure up?

Terry: I'm a little apprehensive about answering this question. Although I've learned how to use these things to be better, I would say that he would probably fare much, much better in these categories than me. But I have learned to bear all things and believe all things and hope all things, because I do believe in endurance. I believe in running the race. I do believe in not quitting. I learned how to not quit, because I did quit. And quitting can be pretty harsh, and pretty cruel and non-productive; because if God put you together, then you going

"If God put you together, then you going against that is going to definitely not work in your favor."

against that is going to definitely not work in your favor.

Marvin: Terry, she's being humble here. Verses 4 through 7, that's her. And then [verses] 11 and 12; she sees very clearly. She's not blind. If you stay close to her long enough, she'll read you in and out. She'll tell you stuff that you may not wanna hear, but it will help you more than hurt you. I can identify those characteristics and, again, the initial question you asked was, "How did I know that this was the one for me?" I'll tell you, sometimes you don't see your characteristics and you don't see your traits, but your mate does. It's not always visible to the one who's wearing this suit... as long as you're in this [earth] suit, sometimes you don't recognize your skills, your talents and the God-given ability God blessed you with. Your mate

> *"Sometimes you don't see your characteristics and you don't see your traits, but your mate does."*

does because your mate stays with you; probably sees you in your worst condition but still cares for you just the same. And I'm so glad that love has these areas that you can kind of go through, because it's necessary. That last one where it says, in the 12th verse, "For now I see through a glass darkly"; It is important for all of us to recognize we don't see everything and we don't know everything... [Verse] 7? I hope for a lot. I bear a lot of things because I express and believe that if I ask God for something, I expect it to happen. So when it comes to enduring some things, and enduring all things, sometimes you go through the worst before you get to the best.

Toyer & Tanya Blake (45 Years)
"LOVE AT FIRST SIGHT... SHE CHANGED MY MIND..."

Q: Tell us how you met or fell in love, and how did you know that either one of you was Mr. or Mrs. Right.

Toyer: Well, I was going somewhere else when I met Tanya, and I saw her and she changed my mind. On sight. I stopped where I was and went over where she was and talked to her. So I asked her, her name, and I guess it was love at first sight. She told me her name was Carolyn... (laughter) So her girlfriend said, "Tanya, hand me that rag out the bucket." They were washing a little Volkswagen. So I said, "Oh, your name's Tanya. Well, my name's Toyer." She thought I was lying. No, but she was trying to brush me off. I stayed and I talked to her. I told her about the Lord, actually. That was my rap. I wasn't even in church though. I was talking about the girls in the church and how they dress, the whole nine. I loved her, and I changed my direction in life because of her. She could communicate, she could talk, she could listen, and she's what I liked visually; and then she was intelligent. She had some principles. So that's the girl that I wanted and I pursued her, in one day. And then that's history... and that was, like, 46 years ago.

Tanya: I was spending the weekend with my two girlfriends. We were doing a girls' weekend, and my girlfriend lived in Toyer's neighborhood – of course, I didn't know that – and we were in her mother's yard washing the car. And Toyer came through, and he stopped and he spoke to my girlfriend, who he knew. And like he said, he introduced himself. So I'm thinking, "I'll just give him any old name because I'm not going to be talking to him or seeing him again after this moment." Toyer stayed out there and talked to me until we finished washing the car. And when we finished, he asked where we were going, and I said, "Oh, we're going over to, you know, just relax at the house." He said, "Ok, well, I'll walk you over." He walked all of us over. I was a pure party animal, and we were going out that night to party. And so the thing was, get the car clean, relax, get up, curl your hair, and the whole nine. So we got something to eat, and I told my other girlfriend: "Go out there and talk to him. I think he likes you." And she said, "No, I think he's interested in **you**." I said, "No. Go out there and talk to him. I'm going to lay down." She went out there and after about 15 minutes, she came back in and said, "He's asking for you." And I was like, "Really?" So I went out, and Toyer and I started talking then. We three girls left. He walked me back down to the car. We didn't exchange phone numbers or anything, and he said, "I'll be around when you get back."

We went to Baltimore, hung out, did a little partying in Baltimore and left to come back to this side of town to finish partying. And when we pulled up, Toyer is over with the guys and I see him break from the guys and come back over. He goes upstairs with us, and he and I talk then, which was about maybe 7, 7:30 in the evening, in the summertime. We talked and I'm watching my girlfriends get ready for the club, while I'm talking to Toyer. They got ready and did what girlfriends do; they left me. And it's funny, because I'm seeing them leave and I'm not bothered. Like, I'm enjoying his company, and we're just sitting on the sofa talking. I didn't realize how long we had talked until, at 5am, they're coming back through the door from the club, and we are still in the same spot talking. My girlfriend said, "Wait a minute. Y'all been right here talking all night?" And we were like, "Yes." We didn't realize it was morning. We were talking, and the only other thing we had was water. I don't think we had any food. Conversation was very good, and the only breaks we had, of course, were to go to the restroom – but just water and conversation until 5am.

Toyer: But do you remember when we went back up to the house, when the three of y'all came back? I grabbed you by your hand and walked up the steps with you, holding your hand.

Tanya: Yeah, I do remember that.

Toyer: I think I put the touch on you, put the anointing on you. (laughter)

Tanya: We talked another two hours til 7, and then he said, "Ok, I'm going to go home." I was like, "Ok, I'm going to go to bed." And just that quick, my nose was stopped up because we were sitting in front of the air conditioning unit and I didn't realize it. So I told him that my nose was stopped up, and he said, "Oh, I'm sorry." So he left, came back with oatmeal raisin cookies and orange juice, and was like, "Here, hope this makes you feel better." So we laughed about that. Of course, I drank the orange juice and [ate the] oatmeal cookies, hoping to feel better, and that's how it started that day.

Q: So let's go into my first question: How would you define love?

Tanya: For me, being in it as long as I've been in it, I would define love as giving of your total self. Giving your all to another person.

Toyer: Having full disclosure. Forsaking all others and being with that person. And that's enough... when you wanna spend all your time with a person, that's important. I mean, I cut a lot of friends back **immediately** after I met her. Places where I used to hang out. She was somebody I couldn't do without, to where all my friends questioned, "Well, why are you with that girl?" It had to be love. I **wanted** to

"When you wanna spend all your time with a person, that's important... She was somebody I couldn't do without."

be with her. So that's my best explanation for now. But love grows, you know.

Q: I was going to say, does it look different now that you're married? You said it was "love at first sight," but how does it look in a marriage? Does it look different?

Toyer: Yes, it does. It's totally different. She's the caregiver; but I wound up being the caregiver, too. When she had gotten in an accident and she couldn't care for me like she normally does, I was the caregiver. And that took love to do that. I used to go to doctor's appointments with her, and the nurses would say, "Is he for real?" They said, "When people go through tragedies like that, they split up; the person can't take it." So it carried me into a whole other dimension. It

> *"When she had gotten in an accident and couldn't care for me like she normally does, I was the caregiver... that took love.*

wasn't physical or a lusty or sexual love. It was **real** love. It looked different. It was different, because both of her legs were broken. It wasn't sexual then at all; it was caring. But as you grow, you'll learn some things. God just let me see some stuff at a young age... Love takes time, you know. You have to put time in.

Tanya: For me, love looks different in marriage because of the sacrifices, because in marriage, you quickly learn that what you want has to quickly mesh with what the other person wants... you end up making sacrifices that you couldn't even imagine, just as a wife. We didn't have children – but if you add children to that, you add a whole other level of sacrifice, as a mom and just as a woman. You learn that even though your husband wants to give you everything and/or can give you everything, you still have to come together and lay aside sometimes your thoughts and your ideas and see what the master plan is for your life, going forward – and see what ***the*** Master's plan is for your life, going forward. And you come together and make that work as a team. And that's not always easy, because most people don't come from the same background. So what you're trying to blend is everything that your mom and dad taught you, with everything that your spouse's mom and dad taught them. And quite often, those things are very different.

Q: You already answered my second question. Can you remember how you viewed love as a child, and what would you tell your 16-year-old self about what it means to ENDURE in love?

Tanya: Yes. I grew up in a largely dysfunctional family. So in dysfunction you imagine and you dream of things that you don't have, and you take depictions from wherever you can get them – television, a book, your friends, your teachers, things that you see. You say, "Ooh, I want that." And so, for me, I imagined that marriage would be kissing and hugging and laughing, all of that. And it is that, but I thought it would be 100% of that. What I didn't know and didn't realize is that deep, intimate part of love – sharing your heart, your whole heart, not being deceptive or deceitful, being able to be vulnerable to this person...

When I first got married, if Toyer would say something to me, I was defensive and looking for the fight, not knowing that is so opposite of love. What I did is, I brought my past with me and would react to him from things that I had seen and heard in my past. So I had to learn, and Toyer had to help me and teach me and be patient. It takes a lot of work to work through that, just on a daily basis. And keep in mind, I didn't know what my triggers were. I was 20 years old when I married Toyer. I grew into my shoes of marriage, and I enjoy them now, but those growing pains, those years... I was the first girl after four boys, so I would cry for things when I wanted my way. Toyer's the first person I ever met who wasn't affected by my crying, so I thought something was wrong with him. Like, doesn't he see me over here crying and he's not reacting to this? He would be like, "Ok, when you finish crying, we'll talk about it." (laughter) Well, I wasn't used to that. What I viewed as love wasn't the God-kind of love that I needed to have to sustain a good, healthy marriage, and I had to learn that. Because I loved Toyer and because Toyer was willing to put the time in with me, I was able to come over to the right way of loving.

> "Because I loved [him] and because [he] was willing to put the time in with me, I was able to come over to the right way of loving."

Toyer: Well, the word of God helped us.

Tanya: Absolutely. Absolutely.

Toyer: I remember she got mad when I said, "The spirit of the parent rests upon the child." (laughs) It's right there in the Bible. It took a lot of the Bible, and then just being patient and being kind.

All that stuff is right there in the Bible, you know, and we applied the word to our lives, and it made a difference. But I did my best, because it wasn't no going back. We wasn't looking back like Lot's wife. It's like, we're going forward; there's no place to go back to. We want more out of our lives than just the norm. We want to be victorious, and that's the way the relationship went. And a young man is supposed to have vision, so I had vision. I wanted something out of life. We were together, and love is full disclosure. We worked on that. We really planned it like that...

"In a marriage and in love, you have to learn how to do without."

Tanya: Lots of discussions. Lots of discussions about things and behaviors and about thoughts and thought patterns and lots of discussions about, "Ok, how are we doing? This has happened. Let's see how we change this." I guess you would go on a date to be romantic, but we would go on dates and talk about how to be better and how to do better. You know, we'd talk things through – sometimes through tears, sometimes through snot, but you'd talk it through and you would practice it. And then you'd be proud of yourself and you would say, "I did better this time, didn't I?" You know, giving each other the accolades – "Wow, Babe. That was so much better this time."

Toyer: One other thing is, in a marriage and in love, you have to learn how to do without. My mom taught me that. It's not getting so much. It's learning how to do without. We've done without, and we saved. You're in love, you better talk about working and saving money, because you can't get nowhere with little pieces of money. But if you put it together, you have a lump sum. Then you can purchase a house or car or whatever; you have to be a good steward of what God's given you. So that's the key – and give. That's a part of love too. Give, so you can have good measures, pressed down and shaken together; that's the word. But in marriage, you can't give all to nobody else. If you got nieces and nephews and kids in your family, grandchildren... charity starts at home. And that's love. I mean, I know preachers have visions and stuff, and then you give to keep the church running. The church is very important, but God is bigger than the four corners of the church. It stretches into family and other folk too.

Q: Why do you think that God says in 1 Corinthians 13 that love is the greatest between hope, faith and love?

Tanya: The forgiveness and the way love will cover... It says love covers all, and love covers a multitude of sin, but love will cover your flaws. You can be so flawed and the person that loves you doesn't even see it. And everyone's like, "Wait a minute. They don't see that on them?" And the person that loves their spouse will say, "I never even noticed that they do that," because the love that you have for that person will cover. It's just because you feel like no matter what they do, as long as I see that smile, see them happy and know that they're happy, then I'm happy. You know? You'll make a place for it, for them. And sometimes you'll even laugh. I'm not saying that you don't bring it to the other person's attention. I'm just using that example. And that's why I think the greatest is love, because love will keep going. Everyone else has stopped and said, "I'm not doing anything else for that person. They have worn me out. I am done." When you get two people and each one wants to make sure the other one is okay? You really get a gem.

Toyer: There's agape love; that's the God-kind of love, like the grandmother has for the children and stuff. But then there's a sexual love; that's different. It's still love – **Eros**. But the love a husband and wife has, you have to slow down sometimes and talk about things. You have to be patient. Love is the greater, because love can go for a long, long time. Like, it covers a multitude of sin and it helps you to make it. If a person doesn't love, they will fall out. Like, one-two, they're gone. But if you're really in love, you can go the 15 rounds, so to speak. And it changes, because stuff that would bother you early on in a marriage, you get a little older, all that's insignificant.

Tanya: And life changes your love; because when we first got married, we had our parents and our grandparents. Through the years, you start to lose people in life. People start to transition, and through those life-changing events, they do two things: They either pull you together and solidify your bond or they rip you apart. If you're already weak, they tear it apart. And so, we dealt with the loss of our grandparents.

> *"Life-changing events, they do two things: They either pull you together or they rip you apart."*

You know, we'd had them our whole lives. We still had the safety net of our parents, and then we lost both sets of our parents. And so those kinds of events – births added to the families, we each have lost siblings; that changes the love. It deepens the value of the love. It increases the value of the love that you have for one another. I know that at the end of the day, my comfort is with Toyer. No matter what, you know, I can come to him.

Toyer: This is it. This is love: It's me and you. It's us, and then it's them. It's us and them. "They" will not come before "me and you." No way. Nobody. The Bible says, "Forsake all others and cleave to your wife." Why did it say that if it didn't mean it? "Forsake" means leave it, let it go, pass it by. Follow instructions. What does "forsake" mean?

> *"This is love: It's me and you… us and them. 'They' will not come before 'me and you.' No way."*

Tanya: I think it said it, because I'm sure the Lord knew what you will need to get through life as a married couple; if you bring all these people into it, you're going to have a big pot of people in your marriage. And I believe that's why the Bible said, "Forsake all others."

Toyer: I've been at church for years and years and years, and I've watched and I've learned. I've seen every man that was in the church, different churches, that didn't forsake all others and cleave to their wife – they were always up doing something in the church, for the church, outside the church, evangelizing, going all over the place, and I don't think God ever told them to do that. Their wife is gone... because they didn't forsake all others from jump street. I mean, that's a message in itself... but God's been good to me. Forty-five years – and I've lived a *long* life in marriage. But I just met somebody the other day at a wedding; they've been married for 60 years. They were still cleaving to one another after 60 years of marriage. That's inspirational to me. If you want to be blessed, you hang with the people that **are** blessed. Birds of a feather flock together, so to speak. I want to be around people that put the time in, because it helps motivate you to put the time in. That's love.

Q: This is my last question: After taking a closer look at 1 Corinthians 13, if you were to insert your spouse's name, how would you both measure up to this scripture? How does your spouse measure up, and how do you think you measure up?

Tanya: I want to answer first. I would put Toyer in every verse of this, because he does this. I didn't come to my marriage with this, but I've learned this in my marriage and I put it into practice. These are the principles and things that Toyer would give me early on in our marriage, and at times I would fight them. At times, I would fight back verbally and I would say, "I don't care what the scriptures say." Toyer, because he came up in church, he came with these principles in his heart to our marriage, and I didn't. But through the word of God, and learning them, and wanting to be holy and live right, these are now my principles. I get it now, and I try to do these principles with my family members and with people that I just meet, you know, wherever I am. But if you put them in your marriage, and even go back and read them from time to time, you're just smoother. Day-to-day operations and day-to-day things are just smoother, because you suddenly try to be charitable in your marriage, think of ways that you can be more loving to your husband or more giving to him and kind within that relationship.

I'll tell you an incident – when we were younger, and we had gone to dinner with a lot of couples from the church, all the husbands were being so sweet to their wives and everything. And I got in the car and told Toyer, "I want you to be sweet to me like that. Why can't you be sweet to me like how they are sweet to their wives?" And he looked at me and he said, "I would be, and I want to be, but I need you to be sweet like the wives. I need you to be sweet like them." We laugh at that now, but can I tell you how bad that impacted me? I thought I was sweet. Quietly, and away from him, it made me look at myself and realize, no, you're not sweet like that. Do you know what I mean? But it started the motions in me not to want to be rough-edged like that, and I'm grateful for it.

Toyer: I was a thug, but I didn't want to be a thug. So love bears all things. I had to bear all that. All that's changed now, and we've put our energy in the right direction, and God has applied all of these things to our lives.

Tanya: He really has, and He's blessed us beyond measure.

Toyer: Right. So, the favor of God is with me in this marriage, and I have love everlasting now. And I have the Lord with me, so that's what's up. I can remember holding Tanya's hand for the first time, running up the steps. Can you remember that, Tanya?

Tanya: I do. I remember.

Toyer: That was serious business, you know, and my main thing was about being in church and just having this perfect type of love... But it's structural. This is a part of who I am.

Tanya: I had to grow into it.

Toyer: Charity suffers long, so you've got 45 years in. It's really good now (laughter).

Tanya: We work on it. We work on it. And marriage is so enjoyable; you aren't going to want to leave that person. You start thinking about it; you're like, "Nah, I don't want to leave."

Toyer: If you married somebody now, it's a great thing, but it ain't no time to be playing around in the times we're living in. This coronavirus is out;

the devil's playing hardball. [If] you're walking around with a softball glove trying to catch stuff, your hand's going to get burned. You need the right equipment. You need to do this for real and don't play with it. It's no turning back.

Tanya: It's so serious though. I think, for me, what I didn't fully comprehend in getting married was the covenant. You enter into a covenant with God, and on your worst day, you still wanna honor that covenant that you made with God. And when things feel like, "I can't go on. There's no way. I can't live with this"; you go back to God where that foundation is. Sometimes you go together; sometimes you go alone. And you pray, and you talk. And the most shocking thing for me was, early on in my marriage, I'd be like, "Lord, change him. Change him. Lord, just move on Toyer's heart." What I

> *"Early on in my marriage, I'd be like, 'Lord, change him.' Change will come, but the change came in me."*

learned was, change will come, but the change came in me. And no one taught me that or told me that when I first started out. I learned that within my marriage. So I wanna pass that on to you, as just one of those marriage nuggets.

CHAPTER 6

DECISIONS, DECISIONS

PART 1: WHAT WOULD YOU DO? (QUIZ)

(The following are based on either actual biblical events or things you might encounter in real life. This quiz is just for fun and a little more personal introspection. Answer truthfully or as closely as possible to what you would likely do at present in the given situations – not what you think you're expected to answer. Select just one A/B/C per item in this section. Then read and compare your answers to those given in the assessment that follows in Part 2.)

LOVE CHECK – Decisions, Decisions: Part 1 (Quiz)

1. If approached by a homeless person on the street asking for money for food, would you:
   A. Give them some money
   B. Buy them food
   C. Ignore them

2. If someone backed into your car but only lightly scratched it, would you:
   A. Resolve to cover damages among yourselves without the insurance company
   B. Let them go, free and clear, since it's only a minor scratch
   C. Report the accident to your insurance company

3. A newly hired waiter fumbles your order. Would you:
   A. Complain to the manager
   B. Let the waiter know so they can fix their mistake
   C. Refuse to give the waiter a tip

LOVE CHECK – Decisions, Decisions: Part 1 (Quiz)

4. You see someone on the side of the road who appears to be having car trouble. Would you:

    A. Ignore them altogether

    B. Slow down and take a closer look, then keep going

    C. Alert the police that someone appears to be stranded on the side of the road

5. A co-worker deliberately tries to provoke and intimidate you on a daily basis. Would you:

    A. Be assertive, but try to diffuse their negative behavior with kindness

    B. Verbally lash out at them in response

    C. Leave the job

6. You find out that your spouse has been unfaithful. Would you:

    A. Forgive them and try to work things out

    B. Get a divorce

    C. Expose them to friends and family

LOVE CHECK – Decisions, Decisions: Part 1 (Quiz)

7. An accident renders your fiancé, the love of your life, partially disabled. Would you:
   A. Break off the engagement completely
   B. Postpone the marriage for a year or two, contingent upon them getting better or not
   C. Marry them anyway at a more appropriate time

8. If you had a choice between having a spouse who had the wealth of King Solomon or the wisdom of King Solomon, would you:
   A. Choose a spouse with wealth
   B. Choose a spouse with wisdom
   C. Be unable to decide

LOVE CHECK – Decisions, Decisions: Part 1 (Quiz)

9. You and bae have planned a romantic night out, when a friend in a serious crisis calls asking for your help. Would you:
   A. Make up an excuse as to why you can't come to them
   B. Postpone your plans to go help your friend
   C. Keep your plans and tell your friend, "I'll be praying for you."

10. Your enemy is being punished for something someone else did – and you know who did it. Would you:
    A. Gloat and/or tease them about it
    B. Admit that it was the other person
    C. Say nothing and let them take blame

11. A very close friend and confidant betrayed your trust. Would you:
    A. Act as though it never happened
    B. Have nothing more to do with them
    C. Forgive them but be cautious of any future communication with them

LOVE CHECK – Decisions, Decisions: Part 1 (Quiz)

12. You've decided to purchase a new car and must decide what to do with your old one. Would you:

    A. Use the old car as a trade-in

    B. Just keep it

    C. Give the car to your neighbor who is financially stressed and needs a vehicle

13. Your sibling wants your opinion on how they look in a new outfit they just purchased, and you hate it. Would you:

    A. Laugh it off and not really give a direct answer

    B. Tell them the truth as nicely as you can

    C. Tell them they look great to spare their feelings

14. Your spouse wants you to participate in an illegal deal. Would you:

    A. Flat out refuse

    B. Promise to report it to authorities if they continue to pressure you

    C. Go along with it to please your spouse

LOVE CHECK – Decisions, Decisions: Part 1 (Quiz)

15. You're exhausted after a long, hard work week but your best friend is in town and leaves you a voice message, desiring to get together. Would you:

A. Politely refuse and promise to make it up to them

B. Make a sacrifice and go out with your friend anyway

C. Avoid answering the phone and don't respond

PART 2: WHAT WOULD LOVE DO? (ASSESSMENT)

As Christians we are held to a high standard and God expects us to love at all times, even in tough situations. This is not intended to shame anyone for perhaps not being as strong as others in these situations, but rather to give us all a closer look at our hearts, where we are currently, and what we need to work on.

Based on what we know about Love and have shared in this book, the following assessment is our take on how Love would respond in the quiz scenarios from Part 1. When you are done reading through the assessment, add up all of your points and check your results.

LOVE CHECK – Decisions, Decisions: Part 2 (Assessment)

Compare Your Answers:

1. **A or B – 1 point**

B is probably the better choice of the two to ensure they get what they need. Money is what they asked for, but their need was food. In the words of Love: "… I was hungry, and you gave me food…" (Matthew 25:35).

2. **A or B – 1 point**

Answer B offers an additional measure of grace, but Answer A is also a kind gesture. "…If you refuse to act kindly, you can hardly expect to be treated kindly. Kind mercy wins over harsh judgment every time" (James 2:13, MSG).

3. **B – 1 point**

Considering ourselves, a little grace and mercy goes a long way when people make mistakes. In the words of Love: "…should not you have had mercy on your fellow servant, as I had mercy on you?" (Matthew 18:33)

LOVE CHECK – Decisions, Decisions: Part 2 (Assessment)

4. C – 1 point

Because of the times we live in, and depending on the circumstances, it is not always wise to stop and offer personal assistance – if, for example, it's late at night, you're a female driving alone, or it's on a secluded road. Just short of offering help yourself, answer C is most likely what Love would do. In the words of Love: "Blessed are the merciful, for they shall receive mercy" (Matthew 5:7).

5. A or C – 1 point

C is not a bad idea, but you could encounter the same problem elsewhere. A is probably the better choice, and the most impactful. It is important to speak up for ourselves, being mindful that "a soft answer turns away wrath" (Proverbs 15:1). In the words of Love: "Love your enemies, bless them that curse you, do good to them that hate you, and pray for them which despitefully use you, and persecute you" (Matthew 5:44).

LOVE CHECK – Decisions, Decisions: Part 2 (Assessment)

6. **A – 1 point**

Though forgiveness is almost never easy, remember that love covers a multitude of sins. "Love bears all things... endures all things" (1 Corinthians 13:7). In the words of Love: "...forgive, and you will be forgiven" (Luke 6:37).

7. **C – 1 point**

This is someone you were prepared to marry already, typically taking on the vows of loving them "for better or worse... in sickness and in health." Answers A and B imply that love is conditional, which it is not. Galatians 6:2 reminds us to "bear one another's burdens, and so fulfill the law of Christ." Love would most likely fulfill the original commitment and marry them.

8. **B – 1 point**

Proverbs 8 makes a clear case for wisdom over wealth, in the words of King Solomon himself – the wealthiest and wisest man in biblical history: "...wisdom is better than jewels and all that you

LOVE CHECK – Decisions, Decisions: Part 2 (Assessment)

may desire cannot compare with her" (verse 11). "My fruit is better than gold, even fine gold, and my yield than choice silver" (verses 18-19); "...whoever finds me finds life and obtains favor from the Lord" (verse 35).

9. B – 1 point

"A friend loves at all times..." (Proverbs 17:17). "...whatever you wish that others would do to you, do also to them" (Matthew 7:12).

10. B – 1 point

"...whoever knows the right thing to do and fails to do it, for him it is sin" (James 4:17). "What does the Lord require of you? To act justly and to love mercy and to walk humbly with your God" (Micah 6:8, NIV).

11. C – 1 point

"Love bears all things" (1 Corinthians 13:7), but "above all else, guard your heart, for everything you do flows from it" (Proverbs 4:23, NIV).

LOVE CHECK – Decisions, Decisions: Part 2 (Assessment)

12. C – 1 point

"Let each of you look not only to his own interests, but also to the interests of others" (Philippians 2:4).

13. A or B – 1 point

A is likely a clever attempt to avoid lying **and** hurting your sibling's feelings, but B is probably the best choice. Rather than being dishonest and deceptive, if you "...speak the truth in love..." (Ephesians 4:15, ERV), perhaps that will allow space for them to make a better wardrobe choice.

14. A – 1 point

"Love is never happy when others do wrong..." (1 Corinthians 13:6, ERV), and "great blessings belong to those who don't listen to evil advice..." (Psalm 1:1, ERV). Love seeks to protect and not expose someone to potential harm or punishment.

15. A or B – 1 point

Though B is a more sacrificial love, A is probably the better answer of the two in this case. You cannot pour from an empty cup. Sometimes rest is

LOVE CHECK – Decisions, Decisions: Part 2 (Assessment)

necessary, even if it's a slight inconvenience to others. In the words of Love: "Come away by yourselves to a desolate place and rest a while" (Mark 6:31).

Results:

Give yourself 1 point for each time your answer matched those in the assessment.

13-15 correct is an excellent score. You are a very selfless and loving individual with a **heart of gold**!

10-12 correct, you have a **heart of silver**! You're a typical person who loves others well but has the occasional challenge in tough situations. It's ok. There's always room for improvement.

0-9 correct, you have a **bronze heart**. You tend to put yourself and your needs first more than you do others. Self-love is a good thing, but be careful not to do so at the expense of others. You may have to get a little uncomfortable and push to love more.

IN CONCLUSION: You have made it to the end of this book, and I hope and pray that you have been inspired, encouraged, challenged, ignited and recharged to be the love of God in the earth, aiming to reflect God in all you do. I sure have. Hopefully, you can recognize the beauty of love even more now when you see it, hear it and experience it. Always remember, God has a high standard for His beloved, with love being at the top of the list. Rise up!

APPENDIX I

RESOURCES

GOT CHRIST?

If you are not a born-again believer, I admonish you to give your life to Christ today. It is a simple decision, and salvation is free. The prayer below will help you on your way. **(If you are already a born-again believer, please skip down to the section "SAVED AND SEEKING TO GO DEEPER.")**

PRAYER OF SALVATION

This prayer is simply a guide to lead you into a relationship with Jesus Christ. Every word must come from your heart. You may speak to Jesus in your own words.

"Heavenly Father, I acknowledge You as Lord. I realize that I am a sinner and that my sins have separated me from You. I willingly surrender to You now and turn away from all sins of my past. Please forgive me for all of my sins.

I believe that Your Son, Jesus Christ died on the cross that I might be forgiven and that I might have eternal life in heaven with Him. I believe that You raised Jesus from the dead and that He is both Lord and God.

I accept You now and submit to You as my Lord and personal Savior from this moment on. Please fill me with Your Holy Spirit to help me obey You, to do Your will, and to experience and exemplify Your love for the rest of my life. In Jesus' name I pray, Amen."

If you decided to repent of your sins and receive Christ today, welcome to God's family! Now, as a way to grow closer to Him, the Bible tells us to follow up on our commitment.

- Get baptized as commanded by Christ.
- Tell someone about your new faith in Christ.

- Spend time with God each day. It does not have to be a long period of time. Just develop the daily habit of praying to Him and reading His Word (the Holy Bible). Ask God to increase your faith and your understanding of the Bible.
- Seek fellowship with other born-again followers of Jesus. Develop or connect with a group of born-again, Bible-believing friends to answer your questions and support you.
- Find a local Bible-believing church where you can worship God.

NEW BELIEVERS

Unsure where to begin studying in the Bible?
Start with the Book of John. Download a Bible app on your phone or read it online here:
https://www.Biblegateway.com/passage/?search=john+1&version=ESV
You can listen online here:
https://www.Biblegateway.com/audio/mclean/esv/John.1

SAVED AND SEEKING TO GO DEEPER?

If you **are** a Spirit-filled, born-again believer, I'm excited for you, my brother or sister in Christ! You need only to draw closer to God to help develop your love walk. We can do this in a number of ways:

1) *Prayer* – The Bible says to pray without ceasing (1 Thessalonians 5:17), so prayer should be a daily, ongoing communication with God. Since communication is a two-way street, not only are we talking to God but we are listening for His voice as well. The more we pray, the more attuned we are to Him and the more we can recognize His voice.

2) *Reading and Listening to God's Word* – One of the best ways to get to know God is through His Word. John 1:1 lets us know that the Word is Jesus Christ in written form. The Word of God is alive and active (See Hebrews 4:13)! You can't read the Word on a regular basis and not be transformed by it. It is not like your typical book, which is only text on a page. No, the Bible is alive, transformative, and full of the wisdom and Spirit of God. It will bring about a change in you, and that change will translate to your relationships with God and with others. The love of God is very much evident through the pages of the Bible; and the more you read it, you can't help but feel His love and become more acquainted with what real love is like. You are less likely to be fooled by a counterfeit example of love that may present itself from day to day. I encourage you to continually pore over the 4 Gospels (Matthew, Mark, Luke and John) to see how Christ operated from day to day, as well as search for scriptures that speak about the love of God (some of which you will find at the end of this book).

3) *Praise & Worship* – The Bible says that God inhabits the praises of His people. If we want to invoke God's presence, we simply need to begin praising and worshiping Him. Sing to Him, speak to Him, love on Him, and bask in His presence! In the course of prayer, praise and worship, there are often spiritual downloads that take place – impartations of His anointing, His power, His gifts and His fruit, chief among them being love. There is nothing like that Secret Place of intimate prayer, praise, worship and communion with God! So as often as you can, meet God there – and let His love abound.

4) Following Christ's example – We must not be only hearers of the Word, but **doers** as well. Nothing beats doing, except maybe being; and that's our ultimate goal – to **be** more like Him. The more we DO what Christ commands, the more we *BE*come like Him. In fact, the Bible says that our obedience to God proves our love for Him. Wanna love on God? Get busy doing what He told us to do in His Word. When we get busy doing what Jesus did and what He told us to do – loving others, praying for others, fasting, doing good wherever we go, serving, proclaiming the gospel, doing the work of ministry, just being obedient to God – we will see supernatural results; a change in our own behavior, attitude and temperament; a change in our interactions with others; spiritual and natural growth; etc. The discipline gained from just doing what Christ did will eventually have us walking in love, and it will become like second nature before we know it. It will also become less difficult to love when we encounter difficult people.

So there you have it – four solid ways to draw closer to and strengthen our relationship with God: 1) Prayer, 2) Reading and listening to God's Word, 3) Praise and worship, and 4) Following Christ's example. If we have the Holy Spirit living on the inside of us, we have the Fruit of the Spirit already (*See Galatians 5:22-23*). Again, love is chief among all and at the top of that list, but we have to water the Root so that fruit may continue to grow and blossom in our lives. God is the Root, and Jesus is the Vine on which our fruit grows; water Him. Daily communion with the Holy Spirit is key.

13 LOVE BYTES

God's Love Revealed in Scripture

1. **John 3:16** – *For God so loved the world, that He gave His only Son, that whoever believes in Him should not perish but have eternal life.*

2. **Romans 5:8** – *...God shows His love for us in that while we were still sinners, Christ died for us.*

3. **Zephaniah 3:17** – *The LORD your God is in your midst, a mighty one who will save; He will rejoice over you with gladness; He will quiet you by His love; He will exult over you with loud singing.*

4. **Isaiah 43:2 (ESV)** – *When you pass through the waters, I will be with you; and through the rivers, they shall not overwhelm you; when you walk through fire you shall not be burned, and the flame shall not consume you.*

5. **Psalms 42:8 (NIV)** – *By day the LORD directs His love, at night His song is with me--a prayer to the God of my life.*

6. **Psalms 56:8 (ESV)** – *You have kept count of my tossings; put my tears in your bottle. Are they not in your book?*
7. **Revelation 7:17 (NIV)** – *...And God will wipe away every tear from their eyes.*
8. **Jeremiah 31:3 (ESV)** – *...I have loved you with an everlasting love; therefore I have continued My faithfulness to you.*
9. **Hebrews 13:5** – *...He has said, "I will never leave you nor forsake you."*
10. **1 Corinthians 13:7 (ESV)** – *Love bears all things, believes all things, hopes all things, endures all things.*
11. **John 15:13 (NIV)** – *Greater love has no one than this: to lay down one's life for one's friends.*
12. **Psalm 86:15** – *But you, O Lord, are a God merciful and gracious, slow to anger and abounding in steadfast love and faithfulness.*
13. **Jeremiah 29:11** – *For I know the plans I have for you, declares the LORD, plans for welfare and not for evil, to give you a future and a hope.*

LOVE CHECK – Appendix I (Resources)

101 WAYS TO LOVE

Random Acts of Kindness

"Do your little bit of good where you are; it's those little bits of good put together that overwhelm the world."

~Desmond Tutu

1.	Listen without interrupting.
2.	Give someone a gift just because.
3.	Give someone a handwritten letter.
4.	Give someone a compliment.
5.	Catch up with an old friend.
6.	Plan a date night on an off night.
7.	Speak to someone you've never spoken to.
8.	Babysit for a busy mom for free.
9.	Donate clothing or food to a charity.
10.	Sponsor a child in a 3rd-world country.
11.	Brighten someone's day with your smile.
12.	Give your spouse breakfast in bed.
13.	Visit an elderly relative.
14.	Give a virtual hello to a friend.
15.	Pray for someone.
16.	Be present when it counts.
17.	Mow a neighbor's lawn.
18.	Care for a sick friend or loved one.
19.	Cook someone a meal.
20.	Sign a petition.
21.	Read a book.
22.	Share a meal.
23.	Apologize and say you're sorry.
24.	Help someone with their chores.
25.	Give a shout-out to someone on social media.
26.	Like and share someone's post.
27.	Keep a secret.

LOVE CHECK – Appendix I (Resources)

28. Wait for someone who's lagging behind.
29. Call to see if someone made it home safe.
30. Run an errand for an elderly neighbor.
31. Hold someone's hand.
32. Applaud someone's performance.
33. Stop and offer roadside assistance to someone.
34. Give a massage.
35. Help someone carry groceries.
36. Give good advice to a youth.
37. Respect someone's wishes.
38. Hold the door for someone.
39. Pay for the meal of the driver in line behind you.
40. Volunteer at a local charity or church.
41. Leave a good tip for your waiter.
42. Say please and thank you.
43. Leave random love notes around the house.
44. Wash a loved one's hair.
45. Take a road trip with a friend.
46. Tell someone you love them.
47. Tell your spouse what you love about them.
48. Give someone a bouquet of flowers.
49. Write a poem for someone you love.
50. Give up your seat for someone who needs it.
51. Spend one-on-one time with your kid.
52. Start a college fund for your kids.
53. Save up to buy your spouse a gift.
54. Name something after a loved one.
55. Choose a person who's usually overlooked.
56. Refer someone to your friend's business.
57. Give someone space and alone time.
58. Remember & honor someone's birthday.
59. Play a game with someone.
60. Go for a walk with someone.
61. Pardon someone's debt.
62. Share an umbrella.
63. Fill up your spouse's gas tank.
64. Wear that dress your husband likes.

LOVE CHECK – Appendix I (Resources)

65. Wear that suit your wife likes.
66. Give someone your undivided attention.
67. Mentor a youth.
68. Teach someone a new skill.
69. Drop some coins in someone's meter.
70. Pick up your spouse's dry cleaning.
71. Make someone a cup of coffee/tea.
72. Make somebody laugh or smile.
73. Welcome the new kid in school.
74. Befriend someone new.
75. Give honor where honor is due.
76. Hold a baby.
77. Give a discount.
78. Wait in line to buy someone's product.
79. Write someone a recommendation.
80. Purchase some Girl Scout cookies.
81. Help someone change a flat tire.
82. Enclose a love note in your kid's lunchbox.
83. Give a welcome gift to a new neighbor.
84. Help someone up who's fallen down.
85. Invite someone over for dinner.
86. Share an encouraging story.
87. Fix someone's wardrobe malfunction.
88. Enclose some money in a greeting card.
89. Give a homeless person food to eat.
90. Help a homeless person find shelter.
91. Give a co-worker a good evaluation.
92. Sing someone a love song.
93. Recognize one who works behind the scenes.
94. Run a bath for a loved one.
95. Let a loved one sleep in on the weekend.
96. Speak well of someone.
97. Defend someone who's being mistreated.
98. Show excitement when you see a loved one.
99. Reward loyalty.
100.   Comfort someone who is grieving.
101.   Laugh at someone's jokes.

LOVE CHECK – Appendix I (Resources)

What would you add to this list?

Share your additions to the list on your social media pages with the following hashtags: #101waystolove #lovecheckbook #MelanieDTheAuthor

Or email us at melaniedtheauthor@yahoo.com for a feature.

Melanie would love to hear from you!
To stay connected, give a shout out to Melanie regarding this book, or share your story of how love has positively impacted your life, please visit her website at:

www.MelanieDTheAuthor.Com

Or email her at:
melaniedtheauthor@yahoo.com

Made in the USA
Middletown, DE
14 October 2024